Better Change in Church

by Rod Street and Nick Cuthbert

Acknowledgements

In writing this book our thanks go especially to those who kindly reviewed earlier drafts of the material and made very helpful comments which have greatly improved the experience for you the reader in terms of clarity, succinctness and coverage of topics that we might not have originally included.

We had the support of many Christian leaders in the development of the book. A special thanks to Cathy Blair, Charles Burgess, Jason Clark, Richard Godden, Andy Hickford, James Lawrence, Peter Mackenzie, Carol Street, Richard Trethewey and Alex Volcansek who all took time out over the summer to review an earlier draft. We found the time and energy that they gave up invaluable in shaping the final product. Whist the improvement is to their credit, the responsibility for any remaining shortcomings is ours!

We have used many illustrations in the book. Most of these are referenced anonymously. We have described these situations honestly at a level of detail designed to protect the confidentiality of the people involved. Our desire has been to show the realities of change in church rather than necessarily provide examples of good or bad practice.

Contents

Introduction

This book

Have you thought about when and how you have changed through your life? Do you know what caused this change in your outlook, values, opinions, activities, job, friends?

We often seek out change. We like to redecorate or get a new car. We like to try out new hobbies or see a new film or play. We love to learn new skills and knowledge. We rejoice at the arrival of children and grandchildren. In so many ways change is something we enjoy.

But if you pause to reflect on some of the most important changes in you as a person and in the way that you live, maybe these changes were not quite so enjoyable? Perhaps there were painful aspects of the change? Obstacles that required courage to face or setbacks that made progress hard? There may have been emotional high points and low points. Even now, looking back on a change that was valuable and worthwhile, it is unlikely to have been a smooth journey from start to finish.

Consider then groups that you have been a part of, especially those who coalesce voluntarily (clubs, teams, social and community groups, churches[1] and many charities) and do not inhabit the formal structures of commercial, public sector or other organisations. Think about important changes in these communities. Most of these changes have probably been accompanied by emotional highs and lows, some pain, and big challenges even if they ultimately strengthened the groups.

This book is about communal change with all its emotional stresses. It is about helping you, and the community that you are a part of, work through changes like these more effectively.

Realising new outcomes with people successfully

Change is woven into every part of our lives. Without the capability to handle it we cannot even survive let alone thrive. In any organisation the ability of everyone to use and respond to changes well is critical – from those who lead it, to those who follow. It is even more important as church.

We have seen so many problems in churches about changes. These are probably no worse than those that crop up in any other group but we long to see Christ's body change whilst maintaining its joy, unity and vitality. To do that, change needs to become something that is wanted by people not just accepted. People need to actively commit to new outcomes rather than just put up with them. Only then will those who engage in it feel positive and energised not drained or beaten up. Only then will God be glorified by our behaviour not saddened. It is about commitment. We need change to be wholehearted.

This book aims to equip you as a leader to better launch, participate in and engage with significant change. We want to help increase your awareness of its nature and provide tools or ways of looking at change that will help you realise better outcomes. It can be just as useful for those who are not leading but merely trying to keep up with what is going on and it will help to explain some of the things that you are feeling and experiencing and may even help you to gain more control over these.

It is a practical book, born out of not just theory but experience in and out of church. It is there to guide, illuminate and prompt. Maybe it will help to explain why things sometimes do not quite work out as you might have liked. It will not eliminate the problems but it will hopefully minimise them and help the pain of change to be as constructive as possible.

How to read and use it

You can use this book in many different ways. You might read it cover to cover – although few people ever do this with a book of this nature (and maybe with any book?). Equally you can pick out relevant chapters to use as needed. Further help and reading, should you want it, can be found at the end of the book.

In the first section, 'God's Church and Change', Chapters 1 and 2 provide vital context, identifying what we are talking about by change and why it is so important for the church to handle it better.

The second section, 'The Challenge of Change in Church' (Chapters 3 to 5), explains some of the unusual challenges of change in church. It then explores the fundamental and universal pattern of change and the transitions that it demands if we are to successfully move forward. It asks those thinking of instigating change to look inside themselves before they begin and to consider what changes might be needed within their own lives if they are to lead church through change effectively.

In the third section, 'Foundations for Change' (Chapters 6 to 8), we examine how to prepare for community change with points to address before launching change. This includes the incredible importance of clarifying the purpose of the church itself. We then highlight issues that may be holding back change and growth. Finally we consider the practical preparatory steps needed for change.

The fourth section, 'Working with the Grain of Change' (Chapters 9 to 12), is as close as we come to a methodology for the steps in change (apart from the summary chapter at the end). It highlights four critical aspects of change. Firstly, the vital spark of dissatisfaction that must start change and then the need to think carefully about individuals and groups within the community and plan to engage each of these. It discusses how to define and describe the goal and finally how to support the change with appropriate structures.

The final section, 'Handling the Tougher Issues' (Chapters 13 to 16), looks at the key themes that leaders have raised with us in discussions. These are common, challenging issues with change. The chapters provide pointers for leaders to engage well with each issue. The first two are obvious – risk and conflict. The others perhaps less so – what is needed to finish a change well and what to do when facing deeper cultural issues.

The final chapter puts all the different subjects together to provide a summary of how to go about organising for change. We have deliberately not provided a simple method, in the belief that this tends to lead to compartmentalised approaches which try to apply off-the-shelf actions to challenges that need specific responses. It is more a 'way of thinking' with a structure that we hope will be helpful in thinking through what needs to be done and when.

1 - Change Defined

Change can be everything or nothing. It happens all the time and only periodically. It covers big transformations and small events. It is difficult to define the boundaries precisely. Yet the challenges of initiating and leading change are a persistent and popular theme in management literature and intuitively we know when we have been through a significant change, even if we cannot define the beginning and the end. So in this chapter we want to outline what we mean when we talk of change. It explains what we mean by the term and what types of changes Christian leaders are considering. It provides an indication of our focus for change in church.

What do we mean when we talk about change

The title 'change' tends to provoke a negative emotional response. It creates unease for a whole lot of reasons that vary from person to person. Yet in some ways this is odd. We find many changes positive. We seek out new skills, jobs, opportunities and experiences. We readily pick up new fashions, tunes and expressions. We assimilate many changes easily and with little thought. The result is that it can be difficult for leaders to be certain beforehand which changes are the ones to be concerned about.

However, changes with certain characteristics are likely to be more challenging for any group. These include shifts in the 'way we see the world', including attitudes and assumptions about what life is about:

- changes in engrained, habitual behaviours;
- changes that we do not immediately choose but that come through our participation in groups with others (e.g. in structures, styles of meeting or places); or
- the alteration of anything significant to us – people, places, values, activities – items that we see as close to our identity, or that give meaning and enjoyment to our life.

This is a wide range. All represent the significant changes that this book is about. These are changes that can create real discontinuities in our lives. They threaten important motivations and stir up strong emotions. When this happens, change is not a gentle, incremental experience but something different: often painful and difficult.

One challenge is that the definition of significant change varies from person to person and situation to situation. Its significance can sometimes seem to be out of proportion to the issues in the specific situation. It is because of this that we can find ourselves leading change when we thought we were just leading.

Types of church change

Over the last few years we have had the privilege of working with nearly one hundred Christian leaders involved in the CPAS Arrow Leadership Programme in the UK. This includes leading the module on the programme about handling change. The discussions during the module have ranged across successful and less successful experiences, illuminating the fears, ideas and strategies that these leaders have encountered in their different ministries.

As a part of that module, we have gathered feedback from leaders on what they understand as 'change'. This provides a practical definition of the sort of events that they consider need a good approach to leading change. Their responses, drawn from a written questionnaire submitted to them ahead of the module, provide a snapshot of church change in the UK at the start of the second decade of the twenty-first century. As the list illustrates, there are a wide variety of changes. Some are generated by circumstances (e.g. schisms, church decline) but most are discretionary, being instigated by the leaders. In these situations, leading change can be especially tough.

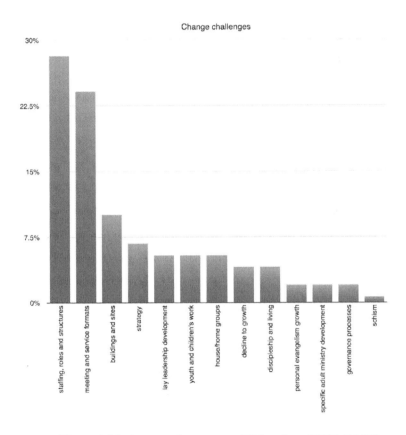

(Note: 149 changes from over 80 leaders 2009-2013)

The most important category, representing over a quarter of all changes, concerned leadership in the church itself. This included a wide range of specific items: from changes in the composition of paid leadership positions and modifications to roles and responsibilities in core leadership positions, to the transfer of leadership to new people and groups. Much of this is inwardly focused, sometimes just within the leadership group itself. In other cases it is about matching the governance structures to the changed needs of the congregation.

The second major category, itself comprising nearly a quarter of all the changes, was altering the pattern and nature of the church services. Almost always this was an externally facing change and reflected the desire of leaders to make the main gatherings of the church more resonant with newcomers and outsiders, most frequently by adopting more contemporary approaches.

Leaders are right to identify both these as major change challenges. In David Brubaker's fascinating study of church change in Arizona, USA[1] these two types of change, to worship services and decision-making structures, represented the most potent correlations with conflict in the church (roughly increasing the probability of conflict by over three times each individually and sevenfold if both were effected in a five-year period).

Given that both these topics are critical to fulfilling the specific mission of the church in its locality, it is perhaps not surprising that they are the most frequent types of change. In a society experiencing lots of changes and in a church whose participation in society has altered so much, these are almost certain to rise to the top.

Something like 10% of all changes on our leaders' agenda were to do with buildings. These were often positive changes –

8

moving to new sites to meet practical needs for space, or to become closer to new housing, or reordering to make better use of the main building. We know from conversations with many church leaders how often buildings are a key item on their desk and how much time and energy these practicalities demand when there are problems. However, in many cases these are not seen as change challenges – but rather the burden of managing an oversized or out-of-date infrastructure with limited resources.

Relatively few leaders (7%) were facing challenges that they felt were strategy driven. This number rises to around 10% when merged with those seeking to transform decline into growth. Tools like mission action planning or structured reviews were the triggers being used to spark these changes. In commercial organisations we would have expected the figures to be much higher but there is probably a broader adoption of regular strategy and review processes in businesses.

The more organic nature of churches often means that they move directly to specific ministry initiatives. This is what you can see in the next batch of headings in the chart – focusing on key groups in and around the church (youth, men, young adults, home groups) and skills development (leadership, discipleship and evangelism).

We sense that these types of changes are likely to become even more important in the next decade for the church. They can often represent a challenge in a different way, calling forth the need to develop something new where little has been done in the congregation before. In these cases there is a need to build commitment and support where no action whatsoever might have been present before.

At the bottom of the list, the changes to governance processes could have been grouped with the first heading on staffing and roles. It was separated out to reflect the fact that it did not involve any structural change. This heading concentrated on change in the leadership processes such as regular reviews or clearer decision-making procedures. Although invisible to the wider church, these changes are identified intelligently as challenges both in their introduction and in making them stick.

This then is the wide-ranging nature of change that we will be discussing in this book: everything from altering the buildings to encouraging discipleship. The common factor underlying all of these is the centrality of people, their response and the challenge of helping them to move through change successfully.

Key point summary

- The definition of significant change varies from person to person.
- Important changes are those that create discontinuity in peoples' lives. These stir the emotions and generate anxiety.
- There is a wide range of change challenges for churches. The most common are about leadership structures and roles. After this it is change to the format of the church services and gatherings. These represent nearly half of the major changes that leaders identify.
- These major challenges will often bring conflict to the surface.

2 - The Need for Change in Church

'It is the church which seeks first the kingdom of God that will experience this constant, fresh effusion of the Spirit's power ... Such a church can never die. If it is willing to go often through the painful process of metamorphosis, and to cast off the chrysalis of the structures and trappings that have ceased to be relevant, there is every confidence that something new and beautiful will emerge which will more perfectly and more suitably express the reign of God for today's world.'

David Watson

Why is change an important topic for Christians? We might think that, with an unchanging God and message, it is more critical to know how to resist change rather than advance it. Yet the church is an organic body that needs to be as agile as possible to follow God's leading and connect effectively with society.

Change – more of it and a better quality of it – is vital to the church. It is central to the mission of the church. In this chapter we explain the centrality of change to the gospel message, examples of change from the Bible and its vital importance in the midst of the massive social change we are experiencing.

Our God is a God of change

In a world which sometimes seems to be addicted to the idea of change, we might expect that the church should emphasise its constancy and unchanging nature. Indeed, some leaders have expressed the concern to us that church is seen as a place of refuge by some who have been hurt by changes outside the church and that, as such, change sits awkwardly with its contribution to society.

It is true that the great certainty we have as Christians is that our God never changes.[1] His word, his character and his will are unchangeable. This much is absolutely sure and we base our confidence in it. But does that mean the church shouldn't change? If the basis of our faith does not change and our commitment to his word and his gospel does not change, the danger is that we readily assume that church should remain the same.

We see this as a mistake. Despite his consistent and unchanging nature, God has always created lots of change and not just in the first week of time. Throughout the Old Testament he institutes new covenants, leads his people to different geographies, chooses and changes leaders, creates and responds to external challenges to his people and uses different tools at different times to achieve his purpose.

We see three important, broad reasons why the church and its leaders need to embrace change positively. Each one individually should lead the church to become restless if it seems to want remain the same today as yesterday. Together they present a compelling argument for progressing change for the kingdom:

1. The gospel message is all about change, about human transformation and development into the likeness of our unchanging God.
2. We see God bringing change to his church again and again in the Bible, as a means of advancing his kingdom.
3. Marked social change is occurring in Western societies. This change demands change in the church if the church is to be relevant to both its members and its mission field.

Not all changes are appropriate or wise. There will always be circumstances in which a change will be for the worse. Our point in making the case for change is more that there is no reasoned defence of change on the simple principle that things should carry on as they have done because some people prefer or expect this.

Change is at the heart of the gospel

Practically and theologically, for us change sits at the heart of being an effective Christian community. 'Change' is so much at the heart of the Christian message that it is almost synonymous with 'life'. Our faith is a transformative journey.

We ourselves need to be constantly changing in our pursuit of God and holiness:

> 'Jesus said: "Truly I tell you, unless you change and become like little children, you will never enter the kingdom of heaven."'
> 'We all, who with unveiled faces contemplate the Lord's glory, are being transformed into his image with ever-increasing glory, which comes from the Lord, who is the Spirit.'
> 'But grow in the grace and knowledge of our Lord and Saviour Jesus Christ. To him be glory both now and for ever.'
> '... speaking the truth in love, we will grow to become in every respect the mature body of him who is the head, that is, Christ.'[2]

Change, growth and transformation are key themes in Scripture. Similarly, as God's people, we are challenged to be effective agents for change in society. This is at the root of the salt and light metaphor: 'You are the salt of the earth. But if the salt loses its saltiness, how can it be made salty again? It is no longer

13

good for anything, except to be thrown out and trampled underfoot. You are the light of the world. A town built on a hill cannot be hidden. Neither do people light a lamp and put it under a bowl. Instead they put it on its stand, and it gives light to everyone in the house. In the same way, let your light shine before others, that they may see your good deeds and glorify your Father in heaven.'[3]

As David Watson wrote, 'The full power and glory of God's kingdom are yet to come, and the church must continually press towards this ideal.'[4] As God's church we need to always be looking for his kingdom, praying for his kingdom and submitting to his rule.

God calls his church to be a transforming witness in society. The sharing of God's grace and truth is always the same but the best ways to do this depend on the circumstances and cultures in which the church operates. As the practical demands change so must our ways. For instance, the growth in the church's ministry to society through food banks is a great example of how we need to change to be relevant. Few might have realised just how relevant and powerful a witness food banks would be for the church in the UK in 2014.

God brings change in his church in the Bible

The New Testament shows God bringing change in his church in several different ways, even in a society that we might think was stable and relatively unchanging. The book of Acts describes a period of constant change as the church sought to understand the implications of the gospel and face the needs and trials of their world.

God called forth change upon change in his church using crisis, charismata and common sense.

Crisis

14

We usually see crisis as a negative thing; something has gone wrong, we are in difficulties. However, the New Testament shows that God often uses a crisis to bring us to the point of change which we might otherwise have not made (see Chapter 9).

There are large and small crises for the early church in Acts. The first major crisis was when the Jewish authorities started persecuting the Christians, culminating in the death of Stephen.[5] After the stoning of Stephen, the disciples were dispersed across the region and they went preaching the gospel. Now if they had been told by the apostles before this to go into Samaria and leave Jerusalem, we doubt many would have gone. But here they had to. Out of a crisis came a massive missionary explosion.

However, even before this there were two smaller crises that also propelled the church forward. The imprisoning of the apostles[6] gave huge opportunity for the gospel locally and the crisis over the care of widows[7] prompted leaders to realign their roles. There is a saying, 'Never waste a crisis.' In a crisis we are often propelled into a change we didn't choose but God did. In a crisis people will give permission for change that they may well have resisted at another time. So it is worth making the most of it even if at the time you are experiencing some hardship.

Charismata

God used the gifts of the Spirit, and some form of direct revelation, to bring change into the early church. Peter had no intention of going anywhere near the Gentiles but a supernatural revelation changed all of that.[8] Philip met the Ethiopian[9] through receiving direct revelation from God. God's action ensured that the whole direction of the church's ministry changed to reach beyond the Jews as he moved in leaders' lives and validated their actions.

God blocked Paul's[10] attempts to go to different geographies. Only once he received a dream did he know for sure what he was meant to do. This guidance opened up the whole of Greece and beyond to the gospel.

The purpose of the gifts that God gives us includes building up the life of the church in new ways. We often miss what God is doing and cannot predict when he might break in. He uses his gifts to help lead, although it is always wise to have these sort of revelations checked with others. This agreement helps validate that this is from God (as Paul did with Luke in Acts 16).

Common sense

We also see God moving the church forward in the New Testament through common sense. We don't regularly have crises, dreams and visions. We are left to work it out for ourselves. This is also what we see in Acts. Paul expected that he would decide where to go on his journeys, being conscious that the Holy Spirit was with him. He regularly moved on when it became obvious that he could do little more because of persecution, or once there was no longer the immediate need for his ministry as the church was established.

He normally started his ministry with those who knew the Scriptures. His modus operandi was to begin in the synagogue but when that was not possible or sufficient he went wherever people congregated to meet.[11] Similarly, when the church scattered it went where it made sense for the individual groups of people to go. God used this.

In all these cases, it made good sense to change, to move on, do something different. Being close to God and sensing when it is time to change is a vital part of being in the living church. It might be more comfortable to remain with what is but we follow a God who is always active in his world and therefore following him means we need to be sensitive not only to what he is doing but also to the needs of the world around us.

We live in a time of massive social change

The world that God loves is always changing. This is true as never before.

We are living in times that pummel us with the pace and breadth of change, generating what Alvin Toffler, forty years ago, famously described as 'future shock'.[12] In the space of a lifetime we have seen massive changes in technology, social values and outlook, appearances and knowledge.

This change assails, inside and outside, all organisations and community groups. Perhaps reflecting this level of change, the writer Stephen Covey suggests that every organisation needs to reinvent, redefine and recreate itself every three to five years. Some will respond, 'a church is not an organisation'. But it is. The dictionary defines organisation as ... *An organised group of people with a particular purpose.* That's us.

The scale of this change is truly enormous. Amongst the most important changes for church are those that have transformed working methods, the communications environment, family structures and social attitudes, for instance:

Technology and communications

Many items that we take for granted now did not exist at all in 1980: the internet, mobile phones, DVDs, mp3s, personal stereos, home printers, life-changing drugs (e.g. statins, antiretrovirals, rituximab), satellite broadcasting. Some of these technologies have taken society by storm. Sixty per cent of adults in the UK now have smartphones. Yet these only appeared in 2007. Broadband internet has grown fivefold in 10 years to reach the majority of households.

In the UK the average adult now spends more time engaged on media and communications activities than sleeping – over 8¹/₂ hours a day. The 16 to 24 age group spend ninety minutes a day on social media and over four hours communicating using devices. Even the average adult spends nearly an hour on social media per day, on a medium that did not exist in 2000.

In the UK by 2009, only 42% of people aged 15 or over read a national daily newspaper compared to 72% in 1978. At the same time over 65% of people bought goods over the internet during that year.

Social structure

In the last forty years, the number of people living alone in the UK has more than doubled and now represents nearly 30% of all households.

Since 1991, the non-white ethnic population of Britain has more than doubled, up from three to seven million.

People are much better educated than they were. In 1985, graduates made up only 7% of the population whilst 45% of people had no qualifications. By 2012 the number of graduates had tripled to 21% and the numbers without qualifications had fallen to 19%.

Social attitudes

Attitudes to sexuality have shifted enormously: In 1983, 17% of people thought homosexuality was 'not wrong at all' in the UK. That figure had risen to 47% by 2012. At the same time, attitudes to gay men or lesbians holding a public position have been transformed: this is now accepted by 90% of the population. It was only accepted by half of the population in 1983.

Levels of trust have collapsed: in the UK only 18% of people trust the government to put the nation's needs ahead of their political party. In 1986, 38% of people did.

Attitudes to faith have changed: in 1983 40% of people considered themselves 'Anglican'. Since then that figure has fallen by half, whilst those who consider themselves of 'no religion' has grown from a third to half the population.

International exposure: the number of people taking holidays abroad has grown more than fivefold since 1971.

Mental well-being

Levels of anxiety and depression: in the USA between 1950 and 2000 there was a steady rise in anxiety amongst men and women. By the late 1980s the average child was more anxious than a child psychiatric patient of the 1950s. In the UK depression amongst people in their mid-20s doubled for those born in 1970 in comparison with 1958 and it is estimated that one in ten children aged five to sixteen is mentally ill.

Individualisation: in the early 1950s in the USA only 12% of teenagers aged 14 to 16 agreed with the statement, 'I am an important person'. By the late 1980s, 80% claimed this and we would guess that it has climbed even higher with the advent of social media, whereby our social selves are even more exposed. Yet this sits alongside the evident stress of rising anxiety and fragile self-esteem.

These examples are only a small slice of the massive changes that have taken place in our way of life over recent decades.[13] We have not talked about many other significant changes: the growth in obesity; falling affiliation to community groups; the rise of consumerism; the emergence of environmental concern; rising immigration pressures; increased life expectancy, etc. These changes dramatically alter not just the context for church but the lives of those who make up the church.

As a result, our churches look and behave differently now than they did even 10 or 20 years ago because our expression of life, our outlooks and expectations, our environment, appearances, activities and tools change. It is an inevitable and inescapable fact. The underlying challenge for leaders is to proactively change so that we have impact and relevance with the gospel in today's culture.

As a living organism, the church must always be on the move. Of course, at its heart, the church is the same. It is a community of love. It loves God, loves one another and loves his world. Apart from that, everything else in terms of structures, meetings, leadership, etc. is really up for grabs. We sometimes get ourselves trapped in rigid behaviour patterns that prevent us behaving fully as his people. Yet we need to be his people if we are to reach our generation with the message of God's love. Churches are God's body on earth. As Bill Hybels has well expressed, they are 'the hope of the world', God's beacon for life in all its fullness.

We cannot be this without seeking change in the church. God's love needs to be the engine of change in all churches. Indeed, it needs to be the engine of life in the church. Therefore, we need leaders who have the skill, the tenacity and the courage to lead us into the changes necessary to align ourselves with his will. Our role is to pray, to follow and to not lose heart, letting him be completely sovereign in our lives and at the core of the church.

Key point summary
- The Christian message is one of change – personal and corporate transformation. Change is something that we should seek.
- God often brings change to his church in the Bible.
- The church in the West is facing a society that has experienced unprecedented rates of social and technological change over the last thirty years. This changes the context for church itself

and for its presentation of the gospel. The church needs to change to best address the opportunities and challenges that this creates.

3 - The Unique Character of Church

Seven characteristics

Leading change well is difficult in almost any circumstance but there are some specific challenges to handling change in churches when compared with other organisations. These characteristics place a premium on leaders' skill in planning and interacting with a broad number and range of people. They make the leading of and participation in change a core skill for the church.

There are seven principal attributes that shape the challenge of leading change in church:

1. Voluntary participation
2. Unclear decision-making processes
3. The spiritual dimension
4. Denominational legacy
5. External appointment
6. A lifestyle community
7. The importance of commitment

Together these factors create a unique challenge to leading change well and make skills in this area vital for all in leadership roles within church.

Voluntary participation

Our society increasingly sees personal choice as paramount. Although theologically becoming part of the church is inherent in becoming a Christian, the growth of individualisation has meant that active church participation is increasingly seen as voluntary.

Church in this sense is a voluntary association. People become a part of a local church because they choose to. They do not need to. They do not get paid for being a part of this body (indeed, in monetary terms it is the reverse). There is no moral obligation or wider social pressure and although proactive Christians will naturally want to become part of a church to meet with other followers, there is no shortage of choices of communities to join in most towns or cities, and even some villages.

In short, church members fundamentally participate if they want to and don't if they don't and they can do this even when fulfilling important roles in the church. There are sometimes one or more paid staff but these are very much the exception, often even in leadership roles.

The impact on handling change is profound. At a practical level it removes much of the 'hard' power that exists in many organisations and which leaders often use to implement change and get over the bumps, handle difficult individuals and generate action.

In church there has to be a higher level of acceptance for action to result. If people really don't like a change then it is easy for them to check out, either bodily or mentally, and leaders have only limited means of tackling this effectively. People can decide not to accept a change. Indeed, they sometimes wait until leaders move on and then unravel them.

The need to engage the heart and mind to initiate change and make it stick is paramount in church.

Unclear decision-making processes
Another feature of church is that it can be difficult to discern if a hierarchy really operates and who is in reality leading. Roles and a hierarchy normally exist but often it is unclear how

much impact this generates, how it fits together and the scope of responsibilities.

This has become clear to us when talking with groups of leaders from churches. The precise authority of church leader, PCC, elders, organist, worship leader, house group leaders, wardens, administrators, etc. is rarely clear. This complicates the leadership and handling of change enormously because it is even less clear who exactly needs to be involved and in what way they need to be engaged in a change. We have found that, even where it is felt to be clear, it is often not when the specifics are discussed.

The human side of change is a big issue and is able to create even more friction than in many other voluntary but often more clearly structured bodies.

The spiritual dimension

There are complications too that arise from being a faith community. Although it is a community that is founded on God's love, it is clear even from the early church that unity sometimes proves a challenge.[1] For many people in the church, their faith will be the most important dimension of their life and a driving force behind decisions and outlook.

The stakes for changing anything that relates to something as important and emotionally charged as this are therefore higher than in almost any other kind of change. You don't tend to see people defiantly saying, 'It was my faith. It's not a big deal – I'll just go and get another one.' For everyone in church change may touch deep-seated values and feelings. It is easy for superficial aspects of life in church to be confused with fundamental ones. The healthy perspective of unity with diversity that is often encouraged in the Bible[2] can easily be lost.

This challenge is exacerbated by a type of emotional blackmail or ultimatum that invokes principled objections to a change. These range from 'I believe God is saying ...' to 'This is immoral ... hurtful' (where the implication is that hurt is immoral). However sincerely felt, these sorts of statements shut down discussion and make it difficult to make progress together. Leading change in this context is tough.

Denominational legacy

For church leaders, particularly in older and more traditional church structures, change is not just a community challenge, but may well involve working against long-established structures, traditions and even ecclesiastical or constitutional laws that hinder change.

Bureaucratic encumbrances, legal responsibilities that no longer align with the position of church in society and the normal obstacles of being within a large organisation can create additional issues for the local church leaders. Change can also sometimes be undermined by the failure of local church leaders to win the support of episcopal leaders when there are vocal advocates opposing change.

In the Anglican Church, the stresses of a system designed for a national network of well-staffed parishes presents significant challenge in a situation where resources, issues and expectations have changed radically. There are few private sector organisations that could afford such a misalignment. Yet this can easily sandbag local leaders with a heavy workload and excessive obstacles to innovation.

This is not a challenge to every leader, even within established structures. There are efforts to address the issues with more appropriate structures (e.g. Pioneer ministries in the Church of England and Methodist organisations). However, these still remain on the edge of church structures rather than as central pillars.

External appointment

In many mainstream church denominations the most senior local church leader is almost always an outsider to the community. They are typically selected by local leaders but come from elsewhere and in most cases will be previously unknown to the church. This does happen in other organisations but it is the exception rather than the norm. In big companies, 80% of chief executives are appointed internally.[3]

This complicates the whole human process of change, especially when it happens at the same time as major changes are being considered. The leader will arrive without the depth of community relationships and with a less-well-developed understanding of the networks, culture and history than those he is leading. At its most fundamental it may even leave the leader on the outside of the community.

This presents significant additional challenges to leaders in their early months in a position.

A lifestyle community

Finally, there is an additional complication that sits at the very nature of church. Church is at least as much about being as doing. We are a community that exists to embody and advocate a way of being and living. We represent every part of society and should be diverse in who we are. We are in our nature and purpose all about love. As a result, the messiness and hurt that inevitably accompanies serious change can seem a complete anathema to the goals of the community.

Change can seem almost totally at odds with our nature. It is further complicated by the reality that many people who join a church community join it for the way it is and what it does rather than what it should become. Naturally they can therefore be less keen on changing it. Maybe this is why it is sometimes said that we especially like changes that make no difference. They are so much less disruptive.

The importance of commitment

We have highlighted the voluntary nature of participation in the church community. This, combined with the centrality of the inner life to the Christian walk, leads to an important attribute of successful change in church. It typically needs commitment.

Leaders in church are often asking for changes to peoples' aims, approach and activities. This is highly discretionary. It is asking for a new commitment. It is asking for a wholehearted change – individual by individual. This is principally an inner change rather than an outward change. This may seem self-evident but it is helpful to understand what this means. Commitment is a vital ingredient for a voluntarily constituted community. Without it, the community is severely, even fatally, damaged.

Commitment is 'a force that binds an individual to a course of action',[4] a positive emotional and behavioural support to new outcomes – as opposed to either:

- not supporting these outcomes with words or actions, or
- complying but having no positive emotional sense about it, with the typical outcome that behaviour is not sustained and people do not feel any sense of benefit.

The Bible picture is one of an intention supported by a sacrifice.[5] Emotionally, people will need to 'pay for' this before the change occurs. This is the challenge.

At Arrow we have asked participants to look at a short list of changes in the life of the church and decide whether or not they need to seek compliance or commitment to the change.

There is rarely agreement within a group but most changes seem to demand commitment for success.

For church to remain vibrant, it needs a high degree of commitment and engagement from its members – overall and especially through change. This needs high-quality change leadership or an understanding congregation (and probably both) and is far more demanding than many leaders realise.

The scale of this challenge can be seen if you look at what we understand about commitment levels in organisations where it is often measured, i.e. in the public and private sector. Despite all the management time and energy that goes into building commitment at work and despite the intrinsic potential benefits of work in terms of self-esteem, achievement, etc, the evidence is that people often remain disengaged. Some published data[6] suggest that the average percentage of engaged employees is only 10-20% across 142 countries.

So Christian leaders who seek commitment will need to work hard to achieve it, a lot harder than their peers in other organisations. Changes readily disengage people. They can make people feel disempowered, alienated from the community and no longer in control of their own lives. Imposed changes reduce engagement. As Jeff Immelt, the current CEO of General Electric, once expressed about his senior team, 'You can sometimes make decisions and impose them but if you do this too often you lose the people that you need.'

In church it is therefore vital that in executing significant change you know how to carry people with you and secure their commitment. Leaders who understand how people adopt change and shape their approach to major change in the light of this will do best.

The importance of handling change well

Perhaps it is because of this last characteristic, commitment, that leading church change well is so important. When the church launches into change, it immediately raises anxiety levels, upsets established momentum and disrupts habits. This seems to be the case whatever the nature of change in service formats, leaders, youth programmes, locations or even furniture.

It's why leading change takes courage, especially in church. It's why leading change is more difficult because it is uncharted territory. It's why it is immensely important that it is led well because the risk of damage to community cohesion is high, and the risk to leaders is high.

Yet, effectively handled change is energising. We know this in our own lives: learning something new, discovering new and different skills, areas or people is stimulating, exciting and gives us a sense of growth and achievement. Even as we have got older the sense of excitement from experiencing something different or building new connections has never left us. The same is true for church.

We need to make the most of change and to do it well if we are go where God wants, when he wants and at the pace he wants.

Key point summary

* The church provides a particularly challenging environment for handling change well. A principal reason for this is the choice that members have to participate or not in church life. Their active participation is voluntary.
* Additional challenges are presented by the lack of clarity over roles and decision-making, the legacy of long-established church structures, and the fact that in most church organisations a new overall leader is almost always an outsider.

- Finally, the church's spiritual focus, which emphasises the importance of both 'being' and 'doing' complicates change further.
- All these factors make it important for leaders to secure real, wholehearted commitment to change.
- Changes are critical points for leaders. They need to be well handled because of their importance, risk and increasing frequency.

4 - The Dynamics of Human Change

Change creates so many challenges because of how people experience change. This shapes what we feel when things alter. It is useful to understand this when experiencing change in any role, but especially when helping to instigate or lead change. In this chapter we will outline:

- the difference between inner and external change;
- the pattern we follow as we transition through change;
- biblical illustrations of this pattern;
- the significance of the steps we go through;
- the added complications of group change; and
- our response to positive and negative changes in our lives.

External change is very different from inner change

> 'When a change happens without people going through a transition, it's just a rearrangement of the chairs.'
>
> *William Bridges*

There is a big difference between external change (altering the building, changing structures, moving the chairs) and the inner processes that accompany this. It is the difference between change and transition. If change happens without transition, the mismatch leaves problems that can rumble on for a long time.

External change is in many ways the simpler part – faster and easier to complete. We have sometimes talked with people

31

about events that occurred years ago and found open wounds that immediately yield the continuing pain of change that has not been accepted and internalised. They have gone through change but not transition.

We can easily become stuck. The end of a chosen job, the loss to houses of a favourite place, the death of a beloved pet – all are events that can leave a person out of sync with their situation. Their world has changed but they have not come to terms with it. It is important to grasp the distinction between what goes on inside and what happens outside because it helps to explain why engaging in 'change' feels so tough.

Change is the movement in external, verifiable facts, whereas transition is the inner feelings and thoughts that people carry with them. The distinction between them is enormous:

Change	Transition
Can alter at a point in time	Is a journey that happens over time
Fact based	Embodies facts and feelings
Easy-ish and technically	Is tough – if it is important to us
Once done is finished, despite how people feel	Needs acceptance to happen

The two are not entirely separate. Many technical projects fail because people do not use the technology properly and don't really adopt the project. These 'technical' projects are undermined by the failure to gain the inner acceptance of the change that is needed for success. As leaders working with churches and commercial organisations for many years, we see the biggest challenges in change with the human not the technical aspects of change. Indeed, even when things go wrong technically these frequently have a human cause.

When we talk about human change in this book we are referring to transition, the inner change that people go through to new behaviours and outcomes. It is this dynamic that can be so challenging.

The pattern of transition

Analysts have identified a pattern that we follow as we transition through a major change. Perhaps the first to identify this was Kurt Lewin[1] but amongst the most accessible to write about it has been William Bridges.[2] Bridges identifies three clear steps associated with transition and makes the point that, 'because transition is a process by which people unplug from an old world and plug into a new world, we can say that transition starts with an ending and ends with a beginning'.

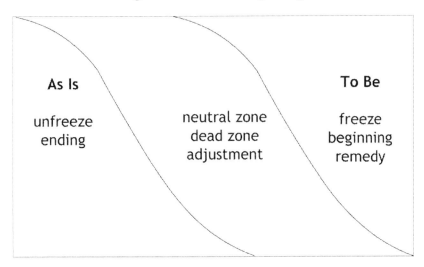

It is perhaps easiest to grasp this pattern by visualising one of your own significant personal changes. Walk through it in your mind, looking at the events and feelings that occurred through time as we outline the steps. Other people have chosen changes like getting married, having a child, moving jobs, retiring, children leaving home, or being made redundant. Any one of these provides a good illustration.

Step One

At the start, we are in a comfortable place where life seems stable and expectations are reasonably clear. There are pressures building for change – some may be identifiable (like children about to go to university) and some under the surface (unknown cost pressures at work, increasing dissatisfaction with the current situation). These can be inner or outer pressures, fast or slow, chosen or forced but it will be these that finally create 'the change'.

They break up the stable pattern of life and move us into an uncomfortable zone where little is clear except that change is definitely happening. The move into this step represents the end of life as we know it.

Step Two

At this point the significance and meaning of the change is typically hazy. Where will it finish? Will it change everything of value? What will it destroy? All the familiar patterns and markers of life become much less accessible or predictable and a period of uncertainty ensures that this is an unsettling and unpleasant experience. At this point we have entered the second stage, a transitional middle step that some call the dead or neutral zone.

This can last a long or short time depending on our psychological state, the situation and the nature of the change. However, after a period, we start to sort things out in our mind.

Step Three

It becomes clearer what the future will be like, what we have lost and what we have gained, how we will get on with life and make the best of it. It is only as this final phase is entered that our lives begin to have a more predictable pattern that we accept what has happened and we really start to grasp the new position. This is the final step in successful transition.

Does this seem familiar? Different analysts call the steps different names but essentially all describe the same underlying concepts:

Step I: The starting outlook which needs an unfreezing or ending, representing the identification (voluntary or compelled) that something needs to change. It is the end of a period of equilibrium and the start of movement in our emotions, expectations and ideas.

Step II: A transition phase, a kind of no-man's land, where things are up in the air. It is a period of instability and movement between two steady states where the signposts are unclear. This is a fluid, uncomfortable and temporary stage that people have to move through to successfully to reach the next step.

Step III: A new equilibrium where expectations start to solidify again around an inner remedy to the turmoil of step II. It represents the end of transition as a move to a new stable equilibrium is completed. The individual starts to feel comfortable again and accepts the new position. This step is not normally reached until most of the external change is complete.

The emotions of this sequence were well captured by one participant in a session who likened the three steps to the experience of a circus acrobat who is swinging on a first trapeze and in order to move to the next one to get to the other side needs to let go of the first trapeze and fly through the air to catch the second. To transition, we need to let go, fly through the air and then grasp onto the new trapeze. Real change always has some aspect of this sensation about it.

This pattern can be seen in group change as well. In one church, one of the home groups became large (18+ people). It built up over many years with one leader who cared a lot about the welfare of the group and prepared carefully for its studies. The people enjoyed being part of the group but as it grew and time went on it became clear that this could not continue. The group needed to split in order to avoid unbalancing the church community, to allow the members to grow in their walk, to find houses to meet in and to enable members to see their security more in Christ than in the group. As this became clear to the group through discussions with the pastor and reflection on the situation they moved into step one: the prospect of the group splitting.

When the group split they moved into step two. People did not enjoy the loss of close friends from the meeting, the change in style of meeting, a new leader, no written notes for prayers, or a different place of meeting. The confusion and discomfort continued until a new pattern was established and they started to see benefits and enjoy their new group: new friends, different ways of doing things, the achievement of successfully tackling new challenges.

At this point they moved out from the middle step to the final one. By and large this story had a positive ending, though not for everyone. For one couple, who felt too uncomfortable and unhappy during the transition, the final step was not to be in a group at all, indeed it was not in the church. The discomfort of change can prompt people to 'check out', sometimes physically.

People do not transition successfully if the discomfort of the middle step is too high and they have other choices, or if the pain of staying emotionally in the first phase is less than the discomfort of the neutral zone. Yet without the discomfort of the neutral zone there is no internal transition or what some would describe as real change.

Understanding the nature of this emotional transition helps us to handle change well personally and with others. It helps us to plan and navigate change. The steps provide a sense of what we can expect to see in people during changes. They highlight the requirements that are needed to progress successfully and explain why transition often takes longer than external change.

Biblical parallels

Despite the differences in the nature of life and society in biblical times, we read of many occasions when people changed their minds and lives. As a result we can see how the Bible describes the process of change, both in personal and corporate narratives and even in the fundamentals of the gospel message.

The picture is consistent with the model that we have outlined above. The Bible shows people going through three steps as they change: leaving behind how they were, followed by a period of transition and sometimes disorientation, and then finally realisation of a new way of living. Illustrations include:

- The Easter story: Jesus is crucified on the Friday. This is followed by a period of emptiness and struggle until there is resurrection and new life on the third day, Sunday, and a new period is entered.
- The liberation of the Jews from Egypt: the first step is the cry for help under the bondage of the Egyptians and the release of the people by God through Moses. But God's people do not then go straight into Canaan. They then spend many years wandering in the wilderness until finally the Israelites are ready and able to possess the Promised Land.
- Moses' own calling and ministry: his life is described in three phases. He is raised in the court of Egypt for forty years. After committing murder and fleeing Egypt he is isolated in the desert for forty years and then he is called to a new ministry to lead the release of God's people.

- The Jewish exile: the Jews lived in Canaan but were warned that their faithlessness was bringing them under judgment. In the sixth century BC Judah fell, the temple was destroyed, and the Jews were carried into captivity in Babylon. Seventy years later they returned and built a second temple.
- Jesus's calling: after many years working with his father as a carpenter, he is commissioned to his ministry and then goes into the wilderness for forty days before he embarks on fulfilling his calling as messiah.
- The birth of the church: Jesus was with the apostles for forty days. He left them at the Ascension with instructions that they wait for the Holy Spirit, which they did until Pentecost, whereupon they then went out to proclaim the gospel.
- Paul's calling to bring the gospel to the Gentiles: from persecuting the early church, he was blinded on the road to Damascus and after spending some time in darkness, his eyes were opened through Ananias. Indeed, after this he also spent a long time in Arabia, before then starting his ministry to the Gentiles proper.

These familiar cameos follow the pattern we have outlined:

- A sequence with three steps and not two, not only a before and an after.
- A middle step that represents an essential time of transition which is different in nature to the final step.
- The new doesn't really get going until the old is well and truly buried. The change starts with an ending.

The steps reflect the real challenge of change: our reluctance to move on; our need to prepare for new things; our loss aversion. The Bible is realistic about the time and effort that

38

transition takes, the fickleness of the human heart and the presence of strong emotions. It highlights the value of marking endings and beginnings and of preparing for significant change.

Intriguingly, the picture can even be seen in our gospel message and Christian walk: repentance is the starting step, sealing the end of what has gone before and marking a decisive turn before being sealed with the Spirit to a life journeying in transition through to the fullness of eternal life with God.

The significance of the steps

What is the value of understanding these steps?

Expectations

They explain the vital role expectations play in our lives. We need to feel in control of ourselves and our environment if we are to remain healthy. The primary way that we exercise this control is through our expectations. We use these to help us know where we are and how we need to think and act.

We need some fixed points. Expectations provide these emotional anchors and help us feel secure. Our expectations do evolve but often, especially as we get older (and so hold them for longer), they do so quite slowly. We quickly come to rely on certain constants that underpin our lives. These can be people, places, meaning, values or patterns that become important to us. We develop expectations that they will be there and we cannot quickly adjust when they move.

Transition is the process of adjusting to and accepting a change in our expectations and assumptions about life.

Dealing with loss

39

Significant change disrupts our expectations. As it does so we quickly see the things that we are losing in the process. We see these losses much more quickly and emotionally than we feel what we stand to gain. There really is a 'bird in the hand' syndrome.

Inner change includes the realisation that our previous expectations are not going to be met. We lose things that we were relying on. These are the endings that Bridges talks about and are the principal reason that many people fear change. We anticipate the pain of losing something valuable.

Losses can be many and varied. In fact it can be quite difficult sometimes for us to even articulate what we have lost. We sense we have lost something but we are not sure why we feel so bad about it. It can be because we feel the loss deeply or because a current change triggers a memory of a past loss, or even because we fear losing even more in the future. When we lose an opportunity, an enjoyment, or a significant part of our life we lose something of our identity.

Resistance

'Resistance ... is not an anchor ... it is a rudder steering us through the rising winds and tides of change ... resistance is simply a very effective, very powerful, very useful survival mechanism.'

Peter de Jager

Losses are why people resist change. Resistance is perfectly normal. We would like to have our cake and be able to eat it. We do not want to lose anything. Resistance to change is feedback on what we are losing. This is natural. Loss aversion is a universal phenomenon. Some economists describe it as irrational. However, we think it is entirely rational. You rarely miss what you have never had but you certainly miss what you have had. It

40

is certainly common. The emotion has even driven pop success with the viral popularity of the newspaper article and song 'Wear sunscreen' in the late 1990s.[3] People contributed lyrics of what they felt they had lost as they aged but had never really valued when they were young.

These losses are why it takes us time to adjust and why we resist. We grieve what we think we are losing and fight against it. The neutral zone is the period that it takes for us to get used to these losses and adjust our expectations. It cannot be skipped. If it isn't there, we have not experienced significant change.

Emotional processes

These losses explain why our reaction to change is emotional and why the emotion is often directed at the leaders or initiators of change. It is why change can produce such a ferocious response. It's not so much logical as psychological.

Change is an emotional journey and one that can cause us to focus more on ourselves and less on the needs of others. It reduces the tendency to observe our natural social mores and unleashes the wild child within. It is not necessarily seemly, nor well aimed. But then a change in one area affects the whole of us and can lead us to express our angst in other directions too.

Losses are forced on us by the change and make us feel that we have lost control of our lives. The certainties that we relied on have shifted and we feel vulnerable and undermined, even if we chose to change. Perversely, we feel this even if we think it is a good change and we want it. Change unwittingly unleashes a Pandora's Box of emotions.

Group complications

There are additional challenges in groups. Although a group may journey along an external change together, individuals will always start and finish transition at different times and move between the steps in their own time. This makes overseeing a group change even more taxing. Leaders can't prepare for, 'This is week three and everyone will be fed up and angry with me. I will psyche myself up for this,' because only some people will be there. Some will not have realised week one has passed and still others will be starting to accept all that has happened.

Creating bridges to the future

Sometimes it is the practical that really helps unlock change.

At one church where the all-age worship had often been led by family groups or pairs of church members there was real desire to widen the narrow group of people who led these services and to do this without losing the thought and quality of these genuinely all-age experiences of church.

The church elders had approached several different people to try to persuade them to lead services or participate but there had been considerable reluctance – in part because people felt that they would not lead them as well as those doing it already.

Possible service leaders were brought together with those already involved in organising the services to talk about the challenge and what might help others to feel able to take on the services. People felt that they did not have the right framework or resources to take on services.

So all agreed to meet to address these two specific issues. The group met one Saturday and, over several hours, lunch and lots of flip-chart sheets, they learned an approach to planning a service, based on what some members had done previously. They talked about where they got material to include and how they built it in. Then together they planned a service.

This session and follow-up enabled 6-8 more people to become actively involved in leading these services. All they needed were the tools, active support and fun in a group to get over the hurdles that they felt stopped them ministering in this way.

All this is complicated further because people do not progress through transition linearly. They often cycle back to earlier emotions and steps: one step forward, two back, another two forward. In groups this can create even more friction.

Our response to change

Inner change is a journey that each of us is more or less capable of handling emotionally. In church this means that it is important that people possess a strong identity in Christ, carry a realistic understanding of themselves, discern the difference between the fundamental and the superficial, and have a healthy approach to conflict resolution. These factors make it much easier for us to not just cope with but to thrive under changing circumstances and quickly move through the stages of transition successfully. Our resilience is a vital factor in making it is easier for change not to become a serious problem.

We can typify progression through the three steps in patterns. These patterns are somewhat different for positively and negatively perceived changes and there are different points at which we may check out, get stuck or cycle back.

Negative changes

It is easy to understand that changes for the worse are difficult to cope with and will produce emotional tremors for people over a prolonged period of time.

Elisabeth Kübler-Ross outlined the pattern for these emotions in a book published in 1969 called *On Death and Dying*. It describes how we respond to significant loss in our lives, the loss of someone that we love.

Although pictured as a wave (see diagram), Kübler-Ross acknowledged that people often get stuck or loop back even as they adjust to bereavement.

Whilst this was first identified as the grief cycle for those bereaved, it has become evident that it is a good representation of the way that we handle any significant, negatively perceived change. In the life of a church this could be one of many things:

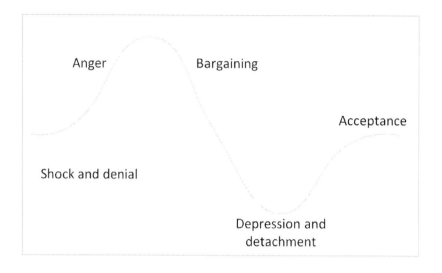

- A significant change in the format, place or shape of the worship service.
- A house group move.
- The ending of the choir or a type of youth group.
- A new initiative that undermines some other aspect of church life, or even
- Changes in personalities or roles in the church leadership.

The cycle starts with the rejection of the change, in shock, avoidance or denial. At this stage we don't really grasp that the change is happening. We don't see what it means for us and if it is awful we may even pretend that it is not that bad or that it is not happening.

It can be seen sometimes on a dreadful scale. The German church responded like this to the rise of Nazi anti-Semitism in the 1920s and 30s. For a long time the church was in a state of disbelief, despite warnings from leaders like Dietrich Bonhoeffer. It could not accept what was happening.

Only as we progress through the cycle do we really appreciate that change is for real. As it starts to sink in, it provokes anger and resentment that fuels our resistance and challenge. This can appear as anxiety, anger or frustration and results in covert or overt attempts to fight it and reverse the change.

Spotting the emotions	
People often conceal their emotional state, especially in a period of change. Identifying where individuals are, especially if there is any weakness in trust, can be difficult. Here are some indicators:	
Denial<ul><li>avoidance – physically or in conversation</li><li>acting as if nothing is happening or seemingly unworried</li><li>suggesting it applies to others not themselves</li><li>only focusing on the present and not what is coming</li></ul>	**Anger/unrealistic pessimism**<ul><li>questioning why (me? now? fairness? possibility of success?)</li><li>complaining or showing irritation</li><li>quiet and passive in discussions</li><li>obvious resistance or awkwardness</li></ul>
Acceptance/looking forward<ul><li>thinking about future issues/challenges</li><li>honest, balanced view of position</li><li>energy for ideas and action, problem solving</li><li>testing or trialling behaviour</li></ul>	**Committing**<ul><li>a sense of control and acceptance</li><li>clear acceptance of implications of change</li><li>emotionally positive and forward looking</li><li>expressing the positives, endorsing change</li></ul>

Assuming that it cannot be stopped, then in an attempt to re-establish some control we may resort to bargaining to mitigate or reverse the change. However, this is still not any form of acceptance of the change, despite how it might appear. It is another way of trying to subvert it and stop the losses that we have experienced.

In a serious change, we typically then fall into depression and emotionally withdraw from the situation. There is a sense of helplessness and a feeling of being overwhelmed by the awfulness of the change. Here is the overwhelming sadness of grief.

Up until now we have been looking backwards. Only after this point do we begin to engage with the changed situation and begin to look forward. At this point we start to see the world as it is with some sense of balance and engagement. We start to adjust to our losses and find out what the change means, to re-engage with people and begin to take some form of action. We might seek to explain how we feel over our loss (and in explaining, we can begin to come to terms with it). We explore our part in the future and test what we can do and what it will mean for us. Through this we begin to accept it and move on but this all takes time.

Positive changes

All these emotions are perhaps unsurprising with a negative change. However, even with positive changes we still go through an emotional process. These transitions too may be represented as a curve where emotions go up and down and engagement ebbs and flows.

We originally came across this curve as an explanation of the adjustment to a job move. It captures the rollercoaster ride that your confidence can go through as you get to grips with the challenges in any new role.

First, we see only the positive aspects of the new job, in the honeymoon period of the role. Then we are gradually sucked down under the overwhelming complexity, problems and unexpected challenges that a new role brings. These emotional oscillations begin to gradually subside as we get to grips with what can really be done with our skills and the available resources and constraints. Finally, we begin to get into a position where we are realistic and confident about what can be done and our emotions stabilise.

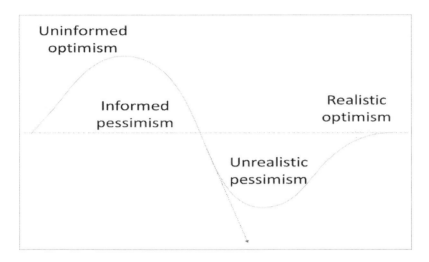

We have heard it described by project workers as a 'wallow curve', explaining the emotions surrounding the slow build-up of understanding about how to go forward as more and more facts become known. This sort of cycle applies to any significant positive change. This might be a new house or location, initiative (diet? exercise?), relationship or, in church, a new pastor, cell group, service, or decision-making structure. Even if initiated with good intentions and positive energy, emotions will oscillate and we take some time to transition.

The scary thing is that this cycle can be quite long. In the case of new jobs, some analysts estimate that it can easily take eighteen months. That is a lot longer than most people would imagine.

Church leaders who initiate change soon after they arrive in post can therefore be in the middle of their own cycle of change at the same time as they trigger group change. They may then face critical actions for the church initiative just when their own confidence is at its lowest point and they feel completely inadequate.

It can be at these moments, when the pressure is high and the confidence low, that people bail out of a situation. They unrealistically lose hope or confidence and backtrack or give up.

You may well be familiar with the emotional significance of change but like us you may forget how much the significance of a change is defined in the eye of the beholder. Something that is of no real importance to one person can be a major issue for another.

We all feel different losses when changes happen and indeed we often don't realise how much store we have put in past expectations until we are in the midst of a change that shows us the significance.

Even well-planned change, change that gently addresses all the real concerns that people have and builds to the future, will need to lead people through these stages and the emotions of the cycles described. Each person goes through them at their own pace and with their own depth of discomfort and capability. Leaders familiar with these patterns are more able to help the church engage with changes well and help people to successfully, and speedily, move to the far side of the curve.

Awareness of this is the foundation for taking a better approach to change and helping congregations fulfil their mission in this world as relevantly, spiritually and unitedly as possible.

Key point summary

- Outer and inner change are different. Churches need effective inner change, i.e. transition, most of the time.
- Transition is a three-step process that reflects how we adjust to new expectations:
    - The change starts with the end of what we are expecting.
    - We then move into an uncomfortable and emotionally difficult 'dead zone' while our patterns of life are changing. We feel out of control.
    - We then start to move into a new period of equilibrium as we accept the changes and start to regain our sense of control.
- This pattern of transition can be seen both in individuals and groups – although in groups, individuals move at different rates through the process.
- The Bible describes a remarkably similar pattern for transition to that observed by many twentieth-century analysts. It recognises the emotional journey people need to take to change effectively. Change is a positive experience when led by God, but not a painless one.
- Resistance is normal. It is feedback on what people feel they are losing as they change. Leaders need to expect and recognise this.
- High emotions are normal. Without them people would not be changing. They should not be taken personally if you are the leader.
- People respond emotionally regardless of whether they are experiencing 'good' or 'bad' changes.

5 - Change Starts with the Leaders

'Everyone thinks of changing the world. No one
thinks of changing himself.'

Leo Tolstoy

'Dear Sir, regarding your article "What's wrong with
the world?" I am. Yours truly, G. K. Chesterton'
In a letter to The Times, *1908 (reputedly)*

A major reason that change fails to take root in organisations is that, as leaders, we do not see that we ourselves must also change. Sometimes, when we change, a lot of other changes occur with little additional effort. Equally, if we are closed or unmotivated to personal change, we often make change in others much more difficult, if not impossible.

This truth applies even to incoming leaders. Once we join an organisation we are then a vital part of the 'who' that must change along with everyone else. Unless we really become a part of the community our ability to help it change is greatly restricted. The Bible describes the church as Christ's body. It is a great expression in so many ways. When we are ill with flu, our whole body feels it from head to toe. No part of our body can insulate itself from the illness. Paul powerfully explains this interdependence in his picture.[1] When church needs to change, we all need to change and it needs to start with the leaders. We describe:

- The ways in which leaders impact the church.
- The way that leaders shape the community's capacity for change.

50

- The foundations for effective leadership – centredness, balance and connectedness.
- The personal preparation that leaders should consider when heading into a time of change.

How leaders impact the church

As leaders, we sometimes object to the idea that we may need to change. We believe the issue is for the organisation and not with us. This is rarely true. Leaders' behaviour and attitude are critical for several reasons.

Leaders are important members of the community

If discrete changes are being considered (e.g. using new teaching materials, moving to a new building) then the leaders' behaviour may not be as critical to success. However, it will be vital whenever changes involves a bigger shift in behaviour or attitude.

Chris Argyris, a Harvard academic, describes these two types of change as 'single loop' (the bulb has broken, we need to fix it) and 'double loop'[2] (the bulb keeps breaking, how do we stop this happening so frequently). This second type of 'systemic' issue needs learning in the very nature of the way things happen. Everyone needs to learn.

This is the sort of change that is often at the heart of church growth. It is akin to what other writers have described as 'adaptive change',[3] a change that requires new values, roles, relationships and behaviours and goes right to the heart of the character of the church.

This invariably needs changes in the self-awareness, behaviours and approach of the leaders, as members of the community and as those with a disproportionate impact on the ways it works. If we do not ourselves adapt then we can imprison the church in the old ways that will undermine growth.

Leaders are role models

Leaders provide important models for behaviour that people tend to follow (this is axiomatic in the term leader). It can be seen easily sometimes, such as in one owner-managed business in which we worked where the charismatic owner almost always wore a blazer to work ... as did many of his team.

However, the real impact is much deeper and more widespread than some leaders appreciate. The message that comes from a bishop who always naturally washes up with his hosts when he comes for a meal (a real example) is profound. People analyse, both at a conscious and sub-conscious level, a leader's attitudes, language, activity and actions, interpreting and adopting aspects of the leader's behaviour into their own.

The behaviour of the leaders (past and present) shapes all aspects of culture – assumptions, beliefs and values – as people seek to conform, belong and cultivate favour.

Impact on the 'system'

The content of leaders' views and the way that we interact amplifies our impact as role models in church. We have a big role in setting goals, in the overt identification of what is important or acceptable, in defining decision-making structures and in anticipating and pre-empting issues that threaten the group.

However, we also impact the church by the way that we are. Communities are organisms, systems in which the interlocking relationships shape the emotions and behaviour of everyone (leaders and members). Over time people develop a way of working that tends to keep the system in balance. This unconsciously defines the roles people play and the interactions that people have. As leaders, we influence this immensely by the way we are, in ourselves and in the relationships that we have.

This is why some leaders and churches can survive and even grow through difficulties whilst others seem to falter and break down; why some issues seem to create massive angst in one group but not in another; and why small issues can create real trouble simply because of what else is going on in the group.

Leaders' presence and behaviour helps or hinders the healthy functioning of the group – be that a church, business, department, hospital, sports team, orchestra or community. It moulds resilience, agility, capacity for change and the effective functioning of the group. It does this by the way that we are and the way that we undertake roles and relationships in the community. What shapes it, as much as how we handle people and change, is how we handle ourselves.

This is why we need to start change by looking inside.

Leaders shape the community's capacity for change

By taking time to think about our own attitudes and the way that we interact with the rest of the church, leaders can help to greatly increase the capacity of the church for change. This is especially true about leaders' attitudes to difference, disagreement and conflict.

To grasp the importance of this, consider what unity really means for a church community. Does it mean everyone must agree? If not, then how much disagreement can be tolerated and about what? Is it not about agreement at all, is it more about a feeling of oneness, and if so how can that be cultivated?

The capacity for change and the true strength of unity are closely related but the meaning of unity needs to be thought through carefully. Too often we intuitively see unity as agreement. If we do, then we will most often halt change in its tracks. Equally though, if unity allows for disagreement then it must maintain cohesion or it results in fracture.

A reasonable working definition might be a shared identity, interdependence and singleness of purpose.[4] This does not mean complete agreement (as some dictionary definitions suggest). A healthy approach to interaction and disagreement provides a strong foundation for going into change, indeed sometimes it can be the change itself (see Chapter 14). Leaders play a pivotal role in this. Conflict resolution flows straight from the way that we 'are' in the community (which of course is often a direct reflection of how we 'are' at home and with others more generally).

Leaders' foundations

What should we look inside for and how should we look to develop? The foundations are to be found in leaders who are:

- well-centred,
- well-balanced emotionally, and
- well-connected to the rest of the church.

Well-centred

It goes without saying that leaders who are close to God and his agenda, spending a good amount of time with him and without unconfessed sin will find themselves in a much better starting position than those who are struggling to do this day by day. However, this is not all we specifically mean when we talk about well-centred.

It is vital that leaders come to change in a good emotional state and with a clear understanding of our role in church. This is similar to the way that in Pilates, there is a resting position with the body 'centred' from which all movements commence. This means three things:

1. Our relationship with God is in a good place.

2. We are secure in our identity, conscious of areas of strength and weakness, and relatively free from fear and worry.

3. We are clear where we stand on key issues in the life of the church, what is our responsibility and what we really control in our role as a leader.

Some leaders have not thought through these things. As a result they can quickly become personally defensive and mistakenly assume responsibility for other people's responsibilities and issues. This immediately destabilises their centre of gravity and limits their capacity to lead change in their community. Thinking specifically about the last two attributes above:

1: Open and secure: Ideally we need to become content: neither judging ourselves nor others and yet aware of our own character, God's love for us and the work that he is doing in us. As surrendered and secure people in God we are in a much better position to be able to honestly exhibit key characteristics that are of incredible value to effective change: to focus on others' perspectives and needs non-judgmentally, to listen well, to be fully present in each situation and to exercise grace ... even under stress.

> 'By judging others we blind ourselves to
> our own evil and to the grace which others are just
> as entitled to as we are.'
> *Dietrich Bonhoeffer*

There is great value in taking time out to enhance this capacity ahead of and through major change when stress levels will otherwise open up significant gaps between our best or desired and worst behaviour.

Routes to grow this are many and varied, with different approaches favouring different people:

- Find and practise the ways that enable you to keep company with God effectively.
- Spend time in personal reflection and prayer, especially on behaviours and the feelings generated in stressful interactions and situations.
- Observe when, and reflect on why, particular situations prompt an instinctive or poor reaction. Trace back to the reasons and begin to plan and practise new tactics for these situations.
- Create an open and accountable relationship with another trusted and listening individual.
- Secure a coach who can help build communication style and skills.
- Hold workshops with other church leaders or more widely to allow mutual feedback and reflection.
- Use diagnostic instruments or review processes (e.g. 360 feedback) that provide insights into your personality and style.
- Identify the individuals who are most difficult to handle and identify the reasons why and how they might be handled differently.

Ask for counselling support if deep-seated issues seem to emerge when considering the level of anxiety normally generated by these kinds of issues.

2: Clear minded: It helps if we think through the nature of our responsibility. Just as Jesus pulled Peter's attention back to his responsibility to 'feed his sheep'5 and not to wonder about the other disciple's responsibility, it helps us to understand that our responsibility is for our own behaviour and not anyone else's.

We can, in Christ, control our behaviour and response but at best only influence others by our actions and our expectations.

This might seem a paradoxical position for a leader but actually it is an important starting point, especially for change, when many existing relationships and responsibilities are going to shift and people will feel uncomfortable. If leaders are clear in this (or at least more clear than not – given we are human) then oddly it adds powerfully to the change capacity in the group because it challenges others to take responsibility for their own behaviour. It reduces stress and undermines misallocated accusations of blame. It helps people to focus on better and more productive interactions.

When leaders do not understand this point there is a tendency to fall into one or both of two traps that undermine leadership in the community:

Over-functioning: Taking on too many things. This puts other leaders and the congregation into an under-functioning role. As someone we know describes it, we 'steal someone else's development opportunity'. This behaviour risks personal burn-out and stunts congregational growth.

Driving people away: Pressing others to behave differently (this is not the same as expecting them to take responsibility for their approach), has the paradoxical impact of driving people to distance themselves and become even less committed to the desired change. It is similar to the response we might expect when wanting our teenager to do something – the more you tell them to do it, the more they do the opposite.

Telling people specifically what to do or assuming the responsibility for their action is not how God treats us. He gives us free-will and expects us to use it to make good choices. It is the behaviour we need to model as leaders. So then what is our responsibility? This is not an invitation for leaders to abdicate our role:

- We should know our role-based responsibilities (e.g. manage the finances, organise someone to create a rota, or preach faithfully) and undertake these. These need to be clear so that we know what our responsibility is and what is someone else's. This can be especially important on administrative functions, as these enable people to operate effectively and not become frustrated. Once done, this clarity becomes a real source of strength. It simultaneously stops the leaders carrying other people's 'monkeys'[6] and encourages others to take responsibility for themselves. This clarity can be cultivated by thinking more about the responsibilities and the limits of control in different aspects of the role.
- It is important that the leaders identify (or develop) a view about what 'I' think and feel about topical issues and challenges in the church. This is not so much so that others should hold the same view, nor to fix on an opinion that will not change. Rather, it is to be more willing to share our view at the right times and to express it clearly even when stressed. It will help others to think, and to develop and express a view for themselves.

Forethought is a powerful antidote to being ambushed on key issues or acquiring responsibilities that someone is seeking to pass on to the wrong person. It enables an interaction to be supported by a helpful reflection rather than just an instant reaction driven by emotion. It enables us to express an opinion in a much more relaxed manner in the heat of the moment – asking others to reflect and share their own opinion.

We don't mean to adopt a fixed view on issues or responsibilities. It would be unhealthy if a person view did not change their views in the face of a better understanding of an issue, or with new information or new factors to consider. This is a perfectly reasonable response. This is more likely if leaders are well-centred, well-balanced and well-connected because it enables an openness that responds to the changing situation and ideas, especially if we have not forcefully sold a point of view previously.

So clarity is helpful and a vital precursor to being better able to maintain a well-balanced response to critical feedback. It can be built up by:

- Thinking through the nature of the leader's role and responsibilities: this is best done in a group and building a picture up of tasks, and especially the nature of the pastoral interactions.
- Looking at critical incidents where leaders feel, on reflection, uncomfortable with the behaviour that is being asked of them: this involves looking at the more difficult characters or occasions in the congregation and reconsidering what is the right responsibility for the leader.
- Listing and reflecting on the key issues or controversies in the life of the church and forming a considered view, understanding what questions drive the view and the answers reached.

This preparation becomes helpful in retaining a well-balanced emotional response to people.

Well-balanced

A well-balanced emotional response demands practice and patience. In situations with little threat or criticism we might find this easy. The challenge is when there is more emotional and personal stress. The crux is to respond genuinely without interpreting any outburst or attack as something personal but rather recognising that it is often a reflection of the emotional state of the other person and a response to their role in the situation (see Chapter 9 on tops, middles and bottoms).

Wearing our own shoes comfortably

Concentrating too much on the change that we want often gets in the way. The more we push for a change in or for someone else, the more that they resist it. At our best, we recognise this phenomenon and when it produces these kinds of tensions it becomes important to refocus back on ourselves.

We need to concentrate on what we control: ourselves, our attitudes and the way that we engage with people. We need to leave others to be responsible for their attitudes and actions. This focus on our own behaviours can often then transform the relationship and achieve change. It is especially helpful when there are opposing groups.

This can require us to tap into a different part of our brain in order to succeed. For our attitude to change we need to believe something different, otherwise our emotions will betray our real thoughts. So in one exercise, a group which had a tense relationship with another department were encouraged to show in their bodies how they were behaving towards them. This was done without judgment or blame, simply as an observation. However, once they had done this and had some fun in doing so, they began to realise the impact this would have and their minds started to change.

They were asked to do new body movements that represented a more useful way of interacting with the other department. This produced a different set of behaviours to which they had genuine commitment.

The inner change preceded the outer, behavioural, change.

An emotional outburst will normally be driven by many other factors than the specific interaction with the leader, factors that may not even be visible to the leader. This could be anxiety over factors related to church or totally separate from it. Much of our own response and behaviour can be subconsciously driven as a reaction to the position that we are in. It is sparked with little conscious thought about the issue under discussion. This can be particularly true in an environment as emotionally significant as church. The result is that these automatic reactions often direct people's words and actions.

Well-balanced leaders are secure enough and prepared well enough to be able to see beyond the outburst and pay attention to the process at least as much as the content of the interaction. This creates an open, non-defensive and playful response to the situation. To respond well takes preparation and practice for most of us. It is not instinctive.

Jesus again and again shows his mastery of this skill in response to tough questions or barbed comments.[7] He sometimes challenges, sometimes confounds and often uses pointed or amusing stories as a response. He is amazingly non-defensive.

Well-balanced leaders are not readily thrown off balance into an automatic and defensive reaction to stressful interactions with members and other leaders. They retain their ability to reflect and detach their feelings from the anxiety that can otherwise be generated in a confrontation. In so doing they help the people they are interacting with to respond with greater conscious thought.

How is this skill developed? It takes a lot of practice, best built up in situations where the stress and pressure is lighter. Practice is the key.

If as a character your natural tendency is to be quite guarded in your views so as not to offend people then your challenge will be to listen and probe carefully and still explain your views, finding ways to be clear without being too defensive.

If you are the sort of person for whom confrontation is no issue then the challenge will be more to explain your view in a way that invites questions and reflection and does not seem to be the end of the matter. It will need more practice on listening

61

carefully to people and genuinely probing to get behind the issues they present. Some leaders master the skill of making topics or questions 'undiscussable' by their attitude. Heartfelt change can only be generated by encouraging the discussion.

Whatever the specific challenge, it helps to develop the skill to reflect on a person's comment (what they actually said and did) and being able to reconsider our immediate interpretation of what they meant and why they did this. This act of reflecting and reframing is foundational to building understanding and balance in tough situations. It might first need to be built up privately but in time the live facilitation skills take the heat out of the dialogue there and then. These skills are developed with practice but are greatly helped by being well-centred.

A reflection:
Think about those times when you tend to react emotionally, and find it difficult to think over the top of the emotion. What are the most common situations and triggers?

Considering these occasions, what context might have been creating the issues for you or the other person?

What specific response could you plan to adopt next time to better manage your response?

Well-connected

The first two characteristics on their own are not enough. As leaders, we also need to be well-connected to the rest of the church, i.e. with wide and strong relationships with others in the church and an understanding of their concerns and motivations.

This is perhaps the most difficult of the three characteristics to maintain effectively. The challenge is that we struggle to maintain both our own unique identity and views and good connections with and emotions towards people. This is the challenge of unity.

The tendency is to fall down in one of two ways, to either:

- seem to agree with people 'to maintain unity' and so lose our own identity and view in the group, or
- become disconnected from others and create a 'them and us' construct that only sees value in our view at the expense of others. This dogmatism will often prevent the identification of genuinely complementary positions.

Unity requires the ability to manage distinctiveness and communion, to see both the individual and the group. It is no good being well-centred if there is not a real connection to a wide cross-section of the community.

When we are well-centred and well-balanced this is a lot easier than it might immediately appear because we will find it easier to look beyond the immediate content of disputes, to see the person and the process without reacting too sharply to the content. This helps to unlock the challenges in disputes in a constructive way and with less anxiety.

It is best to maintain connection with people by deliberately approaching and engaging those whom we know we have difficulties with. We should remain confident in our own positions and responsibilities but equally interested in their opinions and seek to learn: we can playfully challenge other views where appropriate, or directly seek to provoke them to reflect more on their position, what drives their view, and what they really want and need.

We see this as perhaps the most difficult leader's characteristic to master. We naturally tend to want to avoid those with whom we disagree (especially painfully and profoundly) and to mix with those with whom we naturally bond. But this is not the New Testament picture of the body and it does not help people move on. People progress when lovingly challenged and this mutual challenge is a vital part of church for leaders and members. It is the combination of truth and grace that Jesus demonstrates with the woman caught in adultery, the rich young ruler or Peter after his denial.[8] The same challenge is needed when people place too much worth in a building, practice or role that does not fit with the purpose, way forward or needs of the church. Too often churches tiptoe round 'difficult' people without helping them to develop into less difficult people.

This needs some deliberate planning to make sure that we seek out those with whom we disagree and continually seek to allow no excuse for them to take offence – other than their disagreement with the well-considered views of the leader. Not everyone will move on (as with the rich young ruler) but many will.

Personal preparation for change

'Where have all the good men gone and where are
all the gods?
Where's the street-wise Hercules to fight the rising
odds?
Isn't there a white knight upon a fiery steed?
Late at night I toss and I turn and I dream of what I
need. I need a hero.'

Bonny Tyler

Conviction
Many people think that what is needed for successful change is a heroic leader. It is a view informed more by movies than reality, more by story than history.

64

Fuelled by the recognition of resistance, conflict and big personalities, many people imagine that it needs a superhuman to engage in change successfully. It is true that for significant changes, there is always a decisive element of courage. This is needed but it is a different quality from what is often pictured.

It is courage often fuelled by something else that prompts change. What prompted Rosa Parks, one day in 1955, to allow herself to be arrested rather than move back down the bus when asked by the driver to vacate the seats for white customers? She must have travelled on the bus many times but that day she decided it was not right to move. Her behaviour triggered a whole wave of action that ultimately drove the bus company under and is rightly a special event in the history of civil rights in the US.

It was courage, but more perhaps a conviction of the injustice of the situation, a 'not this time' quality that meant something needed to be done now. This sense of moral purpose is often critical.

Too often though we rewrite history around the leader. The leader becomes the reason why things succeed or fail. This is just as true in church as elsewhere as David Brubaker's study shows.[9] The true picture of successfully leading change has more in common with Lincoln rather than Patten (or at least the films anyway) – with many actors and helpers making things happen. It is not a solo performance.

There is courage but more conviction. There are bold strokes but many more focused, careful ones. There is individual boldness but more shared experience. The average Hollywood movie provides a very poor example of leading to create sustainable change … especially without creating collateral damage.

Energy and resilience

Nonetheless, change is a bumpy ride that demands preparation to sustain the journey. There are two aspects of personal capability that are particularly important when starting the journey – energy and resilience.

These are identified as critical attributes in many leadership analyses, for example, by John Kotter,[10] a leading writer on change. They are also topics of conversation that we have had with leaders as they consider what they suspect will be a difficult change task.

Energy is important for a number of reasons:

- The need to speak frequently about the future and the reasons for change.
- More activity – especially 1:1 discussions and sensitive group meetings.
- More decision-making under uncertainty (this saps energy from the brain).
- Good perspective and balance in the face of things that go wrong or badly.
- Handling conflicts and difficult people.
- Providing clarity, assurance and confidence for those passing through the anxiety of the neutral zone.

This energy is psychological strength and confidence in the importance and truth of the change being led. Both are needed as people question the direction, speed and progress of change or bemoan the losses that they are experiencing. Leaders must be able to listen, have open-minded discussions, and remind everyone of the value of what is happening. We have to be able to empathise with people and acknowledge their issues without losing our temper or being worn down.

In the early stages the vast amount of work that is needed draws on leaders' energy reserves. This can be particularly true where little successful change has happened recently and people are worn down.

In its turn, energy is closely related to resilience. Leaders need to bring their own resilience into change. Serious change has the capacity to rip through whatever watertight compartments we have in our lives. It can become all-encompassing. Resilience is vital. Without it the leader's health and balance will suffer and in turn the change may fail.

Researchers Werner and Smith[11] developed a simple way to define a resilient person. They say that a resilient person loves well, works well, plays well and expects well. Resilience is this strength of well-being. It is the personal strength that helps leaders and their groups to manage the stress of change.

Everyone is different in how they sustain their energy and resilience and it is important that leaders recognise the coming stress and secure a good support structure. We each need to know what recharges our batteries and make sure that these things are in place before embarking on change.

What works for you? For some it is free time or time away from the place where the change is happening. For others it is vigorous activity, often sport, DIY or some other physical exertion. Still others need time alone, or entertainment, or time with select friends. Whatever works for you, it is valuable to get it in place before things become too pressured.

Generally though there are some common factors that improve resilience for most people:

- Health basics – a good amount of sleep and rest and a healthy diet.
- Social connections that enable a person to cultivate and sustain great links with others. In addition to its importance in the process of change, good connections

provide a protected base of trust that sustains us when the going gets tough (through family, friends, etc.).

- A generally positive inner sense of purpose, worth and hope for the future – at a personal level and in connection with the world. Even if life is complex, it is viewed as having opportunity.
- A secure sense of identity and self-worth, that helps to provide flexibility and courage in the face of uncertainty and challenge.
- Positive problem-solving, structuring and organising skills that help in both creative and critical analysis of the sometimes rapidly changing situations that need handling.

Elements of energy and resilience are given by a person's temperament, time of life and physical make-up but it is still possible to enhance these by prudent preparation and it is worth doing so.

Being realistic about your own capacity as a leader is vital when deciding how much change to simultaneously initiate and run, how fast change can go and how big a team is needed to press forward.

Facing the fear
Many people fear change. Not surprisingly this includes leaders. It is not always clear what creates this fear in us but it is most unfortunate given that we are told so many times in the Bible that we do not need to be afraid. (We daren't provide a number for how often in the Bible this command is given as the discussion threads on the web go back and forth on the answer.)

Maybe the fear stretches back to major childhood events like the first time that we remember our mother leaving us, or starting a new school or moving home. Maybe it is based on a specific bad experience which hurt enormously and is called to

68

mind whenever a change is mooted. Or maybe it is a general pessimism or timidity that makes the unknown challenge seem daunting.

At the least it can be the thought that we might lose something valuable and it will hurt. These thoughts are present under the surface in every congregation, only awaiting the warming light of a proposed change to germinate and grow.

This is true for leaders. Sometimes it is not assuaged by the challenge, 'What's the worst that can happen?' Certainly in our case, if we put our minds to it we can come up with some hair-raisingly nasty scenarios and in most of these the leaders come off worst.

It is important to face this fear and allow it to surface. It is also important not to stoke it.

Some people think that future pain is a powerful motivator for change. Some change theorists use the analogy of a 'burning platform'.[12] It has visual power as a compelling reason to change but fear stokes up our survival instincts and these get in the way of productive change. The fight, flight or freeze syndrome that springs into action when we are fearful is not helpful for successful sustained change.

When we recognise this fear in ourselves we need to handle it carefully:

- Identify and acknowledge it to help take the sting out of it.
- Face it and explore with God why it is there and how real it is.
- Where it is based on a possible reality (e.g. being called on to lead where we feel inadequate), then create a plan to address the specific issue (e.g. skills training, personal coaching or additional help).

- Explore the possible alternative futures and put a more reasoned perspective on choices and outcomes.
- Get some warm-hearted affirmation and support from someone who will listen and pray with us.
- Think through the baby steps to moving forward: things that can make the improbable practicable.
- However, perhaps the most powerful way to undermine fear is to become even clearer why change is needed, especially when it latches onto important motivations within us.

Truth and conviction are the enemies of fear. Focusing on these can often help to give the strength to face down fear. One shy teenage girl whom we knew moved from being totally unprepared to share her testimony publicly to giving a short but fluid and compelling personal account of her experience to a group of well over a hundred because she latched onto the conviction that it was what God wanted from her and all she was doing was relaying her story as God expected her to do.

Key point summary

- Leaders have a disproportionate impact on change in a church community. Their attitudes, role-model behaviour and influence over decisions make them critical influencers on change. Indeed, leaders shape the overall capacity of the church to change effectively.
- Even if new to the community, leaders need to change with the church.
- Leaders will be most effective in their role in change if they are:
  - Well-centred: at home with God, in their own identity and on key church issues.
  - Well-balanced emotionally: being able to see beyond any criticism and respond to the wider situation, by paying attention to the process as much as the person.

- Well-connected to others: remain personally engaged with those who criticise rather than avoiding or ostracising them.
- Sometimes, leaders who recognise challenges in their levels of openness and security will need to work on these before they launch change.
- Similarly, leaders need to be clear about their responsibilities, and the difference between these and the responsibilities of others in the church.
- Leaders play a vital role in shaping the character of change – keeping it open, calm and honest and breeding the trust needed in times of anxiety.
- Leaders need to remain restless and courageous for what God wants to do with his church.

6 - Start with Why

'Why?' seems to be one of the first and most persistent questions of the toddler. We need to exercise a similar focus on it before we embark on change. In this chapter we explain:

- Why we see it as the first and most important question to be answered.
- The power and importance of leading from purpose.
- Where 'why' fits with vision and strategy.
- How our church 'why' shapes change.

The first question

Whenever change is introduced, people ask, 'Why?' It is the first question that passes their lips. However, whatever reason is given, the answer will only be satisfactory if we have decided on a far more profound 'why' and are able to articulate this clearly. In fact, all change becomes hugely easier if everyone, leadership team and church, are all working on the basis of the same 'why'. Let us explain what we mean by why.

Nowadays a whole mishmash of terms is banded about: vision, purpose, strategy, goals, targets. These terms mean different things to different people and often people are unclear about where to begin. The best place is 'why'.

On any new topic, we start with the questions that are considered basic in information-gathering: who, what, why, where, when and how. They provide a formula for getting the complete story on any subject. 'Why' is about purpose. In church, we need to avoid it being no more than a neat but unmeasurable, unaccountable, vague nicety. If our 'why' is clear it will drive everything we do. It will shape all change. This can be seen with people again and again.

Imagine that, next Sunday, you announce that, after church, everyone will be needed to dig up the car park. You supply them with picks, shovels and all the necessary equipment to hack though the tarmac and remove quantities of soil. The reaction you will get will be hugely varied, from the compliant, through those who do it but mutter all the time, to those who walk away in disgust, thinking it a stupid idea.

Now, suppose you announce to the congregation, 'We have it on good authority that a priceless treasure is buried under the car park and it is ours to keep provided we can find it today.' How different the reaction might be. Not only would people work hard but they would come up with all sorts of strategies to get the job done quicker and more efficiently. Even the weak-bodied would make cups of tea. All because they understand 'why'.

Similarly, listen to the mother trying to convince her little son to eat his vegetables:

'But why should I?' 'Because they are good for you.' 'But why are they good for me?' 'Because they contain vital nutrients that your body needs.' 'But why does my body need them?' ... and on it goes. He wants to know the ultimate 'why' or maybe just doesn't like broccoli.

When we go to a doctor's surgery and announce we have a severe stomach pain, we explain what the problem is. With a competent doctor, our hope is that, although this is of interest to them, the more important question they should be seeking to answer is not just 'what' but 'why'. This drives the right treatment. Relieving the pain is not the same as sorting out the cause of the problem. To do this, the 'why' needs to be clear.

In the late 1990s, the Willow Creek Community Church, Illinois, ran a large conference in the UK where they shared their vision and practice for reaching non-Christians. What most people took from the conference was the idea of running what became known as 'seeker services'. These were popular for a time, until in many places they ran out of steam. However valuable that might have been, we would all have done better not just to have been enthusiastic about the what and the how but to have asked the question 'why?'. Seeker services were just the means that they were using at the time to answer the 'why'. If everyone had understood the reason, we might have tried other 'what's and would still be doing things today to fulfil the underlying purpose.

The 'why' in business and education

Simon Sinek, in his book *Start With Why*,[1] explains that most organisations spend their time answering the questions that start with 'what' (what are we aiming to make or market), 'where' (where is the best place to sell and to whom), 'who' (who should be doing what in order for us to succeed) and 'how' (how should we go about doing all these things). Sinek's thesis is that companies that do well in the fast-changing markets of today are those that have spent time defining their 'why'. Once this is clarified every other decision hangs on it and it makes change far simpler because all changes reflect back to the agreed 'why'. So, when asked, 'What is the reason for making this change?' the answer is that it helps us to fulfil our 'why' better. The why, or purpose, shapes the where (vision), the how (strategy) and the who (people).

He illustrates this with the success of Apple. He surmises that if Apple were like most other producers their marketing message might read: 'We make great computers. They're beautifully designed, simple to use and user-friendly. Wanna buy one?' Yet in fact they communicate starting with the why not the what: 'In everything we do, we believe in challenging the status

74

quo. We believe in thinking differently. The way we challenge the status quo is by making our products beautifully designed, simple to use and user-friendly. We happen to make great computers. Wanna buy one?' Why is powerful.

In a recent large and somewhat controversial national infrastructure project, the chairman produced an extensive report to lay out the basis of the scheme. He began with these words: 'The biggest danger in any major project is losing sight of why you are doing it in the first place. Why is it worth the effort, not to mention the cost? What is the problem that it is the answer to? What is the core purpose you are trying to achieve? Those questions, and that clarity, are particularly relevant for a project of the size, duration, complexity, impact and cost of this one. Why is it worth the effort? What is the key problem that it is trying to address? What is its key purpose?'

Michael Fullan,[2] who writes primarily in the context of education, says that when trying to raise the standards in teaching and in the learning environment of schools, the key is not just methods, materials and training. He observes that you will only really bring about real change if you have what he calls 'moral purpose', in other words, a guiding belief that drives everything else and upon which every change is made. It is the compass reading for all change and determines success or failure. This guiding belief or moral purpose defines the 'why' on which everything else is built.

The church and 'why'

Now, where does the church fit into this? We often attend conferences and read books in order to improve the way our church does things. We focus on the what, the how and the who. We want a quick fix. We grab a model off someone else's shelf and try to apply it, wondering later why it didn't work as well as seemingly promised. However good, however tried and tested, and however brilliant the writers and speakers, ideas are always difficult to implement if we do not have a well-accepted 'why' founded on a strongly held belief.

Too often, church leaders can explain in great detail about what the church does. Often the more it does the more impressive it sounds. They can be clear on the how and who does it. But when asked 'why' the answer may be far less clear.

Messy integration?

Many churches have embraced the whole idea of engaging families with 'Messy Church' and testify to the attractiveness and value of the initiative. But probing the 'why' of Messy Church has led some to think more widely about what is actually needed in drawing families into Christian discipleship.

One church, as it looked at Messy Church, became concerned that it would become like a 'revolving door' for families coming into and then growing out of a certain life stage. It has crafted additional changes in its programmes to, for instance, encourage social activities that enable attendees to meet and become friends with other church members and pick up on other activities that build ongoing church participation.

Leaders have a 'why' but it is rarely vocalised or put down on paper. Yet when a church defines itself by what it does, it is difficult to make changes. If it is intentional about its activity and clear about why then, as circumstances change, it will be freer to respond effectively, dropping less relevant activities and putting in place more appropriate ones.

One of the reasons that churches find themselves on a plateau or sliding down the growth curve is that they have lost touch with their 'why'. They are so consumed with what they are doing that they have forgotten the real drivers for all these activities.

Those who pioneer churches are consumed with a purpose. They don't initially care how they do it or what it takes as long as they can achieve their purpose. Once a church is established people often join because they like what the church offers. In fact, churches often advertise themselves on the basis of the goods available.

The 'what' attracts interest. Yet it is the 'why' that attracts passion. 'What' attracts consumers. 'Why' attracts disciples. 'What' creates attraction which is easily lost. 'Why' creates loyalty which is hard to lose.

If we give people what they want, we will usually end up being ineffective but if we ask why, then we may end up being very creative. As Henry Ford said, 'If I had given people what they wanted, they would have said a faster horse.'

If your church has a mission statement that is trite and meaningless to most people, then when it comes to making changes, the answer to the question why will only be answered with reference to the immediate need and not the real purpose of the church. Yet this misses the most powerful tool for being strategic and enabling change. A mission or purpose statement that expresses the passion of the heart is liberating. Too often it is left to be meaningless and ineffective.

Leading from purpose

It cannot be said too strongly that being really clear about why the church exists is powerful and can affect everything we do in church life. It gives permission to start, not start or stop activities. It is the foundation for, and will directly shape, any vision and strategy.

Sadly many churches are unclear about their ultimate purpose. This is not a comment on whether they have a 'mission statement' or not. It is about whether they have a burning compulsion in their heart about God and the local church that shapes everything they seek to do. Activities can be more or less effective for many reasons but the key for long-term, sustainable effectiveness is to be clear about 'why'.

If on our websites and in our descriptions of the church we emphasise what we do and who we are, people will respond to this. That is the best way to attract consumers – looking for the what. They will seek the best 'what' near them. But if we focus on not just what we do but the passion that drives us, then those attracted would come because they relate to our heart and passion. If they join because of that, they are going to be less worried when we make changes because they know that changes have to be made to be fruitful in achieving our 'why'.

Clarity about the 'why' enables us to differentiate the fundamental from the superficial much more clearly. Consumers complain when the 'what's are changed because that is why they came in the first place.

The impact can be profound. When you advertise for a new post in the church, do you share the what or the why? Which is more useful: 'Children's pastor needed in growing church. Qualifications required: love for children, good organisation skills, good team player. Experience essential.' Or, 'This church believes that God loves children and wants them to come to know him and grow up as disciples of Jesus. If you share this passion, we are looking for a children's worker. We need you to love children, have good organisational skills …'?

Vision vs purpose: where vs why

A frequent misconception, that we can be burdened with as leaders, is that leading is first and foremost about vision, about where we are headed and the shape and detail of this. Some see the start of change as being about setting the vision. This is not the best place to start. Vision does not even need to come from the leader. The best place to start is the 'why'.

If we are not clear why we exist, how can we possibly decide where to go or what we should be doing? Our underlying purpose needs to be the driving force behind whatever the what and where will be.

Let's start, though, by being clear what we mean and go back to definitions and distinguish between purpose and vision, why and where.

The dictionary defines vision in terms of a future image (see inset). In other words it answers the questions, 'Where do we think we are going?', 'Where do we think we will be in a few years?' (See Chapter 10 for more on vision.) Similarly, the dictionary defines purpose in terms that are all about 'why'.

> **Vision** *noun*
> The ability to think about or plan the future with imagination or wisdom. A mental image of what the future will or could be like. A vivid mental image.
> **Purpose** *noun*
> The reason for which something is done or created or for which something exists. Have as one's intention or objective.
> *Online Oxford Dictionary, OUP*

So, we suggest, alongside familiar words such as purpose, vision, strategy, you put words that actually define what you mean, i.e., Why, Where, Who and What. When you are as clear as you can be about vision (where), you can work out the path to the changes necessary to get you there. Your strategy (what) will reflect those changes, but all of it will be undergirded by a motivational belief and a clear purpose (why) and this is the place to begin. We often work with church leaders through four questions:

1. What is God's why for your church?
2. What is the leaders' why for the church?

3. What do the congregation believe to be the why for the church? and
4. What do the local community believe is the why of the church?

The key is to establish clarity on the answers to these questions and then begin to align them so that at least the top three are in agreement. Everything should line up with God's 'why'. He blesses what he initiates and we will save huge amounts of time and energy if we are clear about his purpose. Our experience is that in many churches, the members and the leaders are not aligned. Part of the long-term aim of being church is to help align these with God's heart. Only what he builds is worth building.[3]

A fifth question

Behind all these questions, there is another fundamental question to be answered: What is your guiding belief about God and the nature of his work in the world? This will be reflected in how you see the role of the local church and the 'why' of its existence. Answering this will set a powerful foundation.

There are many variations and possibilities. Each one shapes what is the primary purpose of the local church because whatever else, it must be that the church is called to do the will of God on earth. What do you believe it is?

From the answer to this, it becomes possible to find the specific 'why' for the church. This must be shaped by the leaders, because a church must be led from passion and this can't be done without believing in the purpose. For each of us, it must reflect the why of God in our area, the primary motivations in the heart of God for our church now.

Some churches have drawn from Jesus' commission, 'As you go, make disciples, baptising them ...'[4] and as they thought this through they have come up with thoughts like,

---

Intentional church

The importance of questioning the 'why' both of church and people's motives for their involvement in the community was brought home in a discussion that we participated in with several ministers operating in small rural church communities.

The group quickly got on to the subject of parishioners' reluctance to change. 'Many have retired to this area, specifically to get away from the changes they see elsewhere,' was typical of the comments. One shared a conversation that had included the sentiment that, 'Things are OK. I have only 5-10 years left and this church will see me out.'

In challenging this attitude, which had caused many obstacles to change and growth, one minister shared the importance and value of getting people to reflect on why the church was important to them, what role it had to play for this to remain the case, and what would be lost if it really did not carry on beyond that 5-10 years.

The discussion had caused a great deal of reflection and generated a much more positive spirit in the congregation to help to ensure that the church would continue to fulfil its role now and into the next generation.

'Our church exists to make disciples of Jesus and help them to grow like him,' and 'Our church exists to make lifelong followers of Jesus.' They may seem terse but these short phrases express their moral purpose and provide a rich platform for proactive work to fulfil the purpose, for encouraging, engaging and challenging the church and for shaping direction and strategy. The discussion that produced them is a rich one that is called forth whenever the phrase is considered. As with lots of forms of planning, the real value is in the planning as much as the plan.

> **The motivating power of purpose**
> A year or so ago, a group of us gave out gifts on Easter Saturday in our local farmers' market. Nobody asked what we were doing. It was pretty obvious. But many asked, 'Why are you doing this?' The what was handing out flowers and gifts. The answer to the why was that we believe God loves the people in our area and wants them to know that Easter is good news for them.

How the why shapes change

Answering the fundamental 'why' of the church is a powerful lever when it comes to change. As leaders, when we initiate change, we will be asked why it is necessary. For the answer to carry legitimacy and weight it needs to track back to a clearly understood purpose for being church there, now. Otherwise it can be a struggle.

For example, if we want to take the pews out of the building and replace them with chairs (a task not to be undertaken lightly), then when asked why, our reply might be that they are more comfortable. The debate might ensue that they have served previous generations well so why change now. It's a lot of money and we have managed up to now. After all, it is only for an hour. If our main purpose is to share Jesus with those outside and our research shows that pews are a deterrent to people coming to a service, they might not like the change but would have to agree that it is a wise decision. We might remind them that in no other circumstance would they invite a friend to an event and make them sit on benches for over an hour.

The illustration is not entirely light-hearted and the rationale is supported by others. Diana Butler Bass[5] studied the growth of churches in the USA. She identified the importance of practising an intentional form of church if they are to find their core meaning in a rapidly changing context. In short, these congregations had identified their why and it shaped their

82

activities and direction. This creates a world of difference. A church with its eyes on the advance of God's kingdom is a different place for change from one concerned about other things.

The man with the green umbrella

Some years ago we visited a large mega-church in the USA. We arrived early for the first service of the day at 8am and parked on the far side of a huge car park. It had been raining quite heavily but as we got out of the car we were greeted by a cheery guy brandishing a green umbrella. He kindly walked us to the building so we arrived relatively dry. In conversation across the car park we had introduced ourselves but, as we parted, we asked him how often he did this. He replied, 'Every Sunday morning. I do the eight o'clock shift.' We then asked him why he did this and without a moment's hesitation he said something along the lines of, 'We are wanting unchurched people to become followers of Jesus.'

Now, what had that got to do with walking people with an umbrella? Everything. He not only knew the why, but it was part of his thinking and his vision; he understood his part in it. He did what he did wholeheartedly because he knew it was a part of the ultimate purpose of the church he belonged to. Almost from its inception, this particular church has had its 'Why' clear and communicated to all: 'This church exists to help turn irreligious people into fully devoted followers of Jesus Christ.' It is based on a core belief: people matter to God; therefore they matter to us. Jesus came to redeem this broken world, both for all eternity and in the here and now. This conviction drives our mission.

You may have a different core belief but, whether you like it or not, it drives what you do. Own it and let it determine your purpose. It will then shape what you do from then on and enable you to bring about change along the way.

Key point summary

- Answering your church's 'why?' first generates the passion, focus and foundation for change.
- Leading into change needs to start from purpose. Visions often identity goals but fail to address the reasoning behind these. Vision needs to follow purpose.
- The intentionality of church is a vital starting point for effective change. This requires the church being clear about its specific purpose.
- It is easy for leaders to build patterns for their church from what they see elsewhere. Yet this can miss the primary need to be clear both about why the church really exists where it is and why a change is needed. These provide the guide for developing the most relevant pattern for a church.
- Collective clarity on the unique purpose of the church community will challenge activities, behaviour and priorities.

7 - Look for Growth Barriers

'Growth is the only evidence of life.'
Cardinal John Henry Newman

Growth is a common focus in business, education and life. It should be similarly central to our Christian faith. We should desire growth both individually and corporately and seek to remove any barriers that might prevent it. God seeks to grow his kingdom and restore his creation to himself. His church is an important instrument for achieving this aim. Yet growth itself demands change.

In this chapter we identify six of the most common barriers to church growth and discuss the importance of addressing these early in order to promote healthy church development.

Growth defined

As a living organism, we would expect the church to grow. Change creates growth and growth generates the need for change. Every parent recognises this. As children grow they change. They change physically, emotionally and intellectually. These changes require careful parental handling. Without adequate and appropriate changes, growth is stunted. The same is true for churches.

Growth in terms of church life means both numerical growth and growth in maturity, holiness and Christlikeness. These different aspects should go naturally together. As Stevens and Collins, writing about the pastor's role, say, we should expect, 'growth into unity, into maturity as a community, into individual theological maturity so members are able to distinguish truth from error for themselves, in love motivated truth speaking, dependence on Christ, the head of the church, and in mutual enrichment'.[1]

It is rather too easy to see growth only in terms of numbers in one place. However, this is not necessarily the best measure. Just as, in the natural world, plants and trees have their maximum size, there will be some churches that are large and some that are small by virtue of where they are and their ministry. One is not superior to the other. Both should be able to grow numerically and not just by means of attracting people from other churches, but some may stay as one large church; others will be planting churches or growing in other ways. Both should grow into greater maturity.

The Bible makes it clear that growth comes from God.[2] We don't create it but we can help to provide an environment in which it will happen more readily and we can certainly do things that will prevent or hinder it. This means we need to be vigilant in looking for barriers to growth.

Growing churches

There is a pattern to growth. Organisations, movements, empires, companies and all living things including human life follow this pattern. Things are born, grow, plateau, then decline and die. So it is naturally true of churches or areas of ministry within a church, if left without intervention.

Charles Handy drew attention to this when he described change in terms of an S-shaped or sigmoid curve[3] (see diagram). He pointed out that organisations can overcome the decline phase if they make changes before the plateau (at point a on the curve). He also pointed out how hard this is to do because it means that you are changing when everything still looks as if it is going really well: you are still in growth and it is difficult to know where you are on the upward curve.

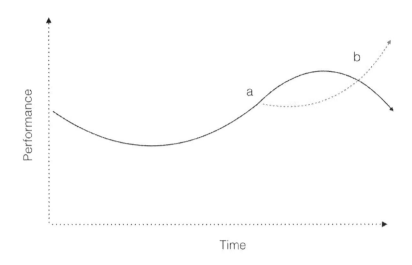

Since most people have no idea when growth will become decline, we are fortunate if we can get it right. We typically think about change only when we notice things plateauing or declining. It is not too late then but much harder and more drastic action is needed.

If we think of organisations in terms of their vision, community, programmes and management, vision and community tend to be the main drivers of growth in the upward phase. However, as organisations mature, programmes and management come to dominate and tend to remain dominant on the downward curve.

When a church begins, it is propelled forward by a community with a vision. Things are driven by a passionate vision of the future held by the community. Those things that distract or weigh the community down are readily discarded in the wake of faith, unity and the hope of the vision. All too quickly, programmes are created to structure the growth, and management to organise it. These slowly but surely come to dominate activities and the others diminish. So a busy church programme with great management can easily be a church in

87

decline without realising it. The way out is to reconnect with purpose and vision and find people who will carry it. This requires courageous change.

Another dynamic that drives these trends is that as churches grow they acquire others who join, not because of the vision but because they are attracted by the programmes, life and benefits that these bring to their family. They are primarily 'consumers'. This dilutes the vision and so begins to alter the culture of the church. It is gradual and often the effects are not recognised until the church plateaus or begins to decline.

Too often, when the vision fades and the environment needs change, the structures, programmes and management carry on regardless and consume everyone's energy. Few see the need amidst the increased activity and busy-ness of church and if they seek change they find serious resistance to changing things that are 'working well'.

Sometimes the church escapes, through a rapid turnover of people (e.g. a student church in a university town where a large part of the congregation moves on each year), a timely injection of new leadership or a significant crisis. More typically though, without bold leadership it will continue until the challenge of decline generates momentum to change. If the church is to avoid a long, gradual decline, a new curve needs to be generated with new passion and vision. As Charles Handy identifies, this will cause a period of disruption and confusion as old and new wrestle for control (hence the shape of the curve from points a to b).

This is why leadership requires courage. As someone once said, 'Fear marks the outer boundaries of the church.' Originally said in the context of sharing our faith, it is just as true in church leadership. Too often, we pay too much attention to the potential loss of members who will baulk at change and at the disruption and personal pain that will be created. It is so much easier to decline slowly rather than seek to grow. Fear always calls us back to the safety of where and what we know.

Common barriers to growth

The sigmoid curve illustrates the sclerosis to which all organisations are naturally vulnerable as they grow. Methods, structures and thinking patterns become familiar. Because they worked well in years gone by, they are retained even if they are less suitable to the current position of the church. These patterns become barriers that hinder the future growth of the church.

Sometimes, if we just remove the barriers to growth, we will be surprised at what God can do. So, let's now look at six of the most common barriers that hinder growth. They represent the glass ceilings to growth and effectiveness. In each case, if a barrier is removed, it may allow the church to shift to a new curve.

These common hindrances arise in leadership, structures, buildings, focus, belonging and culture.

Leadership

We all (including leaders) have expectations of the leaders in our church. These expectations can become a hindrance to growth as the congregation starts to grow, especially past the 120-150 mark (although it can be much earlier depending on the individual and context). Expectations are often unspoken but can be deeply engrained from previous experience. Typically, in the Anglican church, the incumbent is viewed as the one through whom all decisions must pass, to whom everyone reports and by whom all serious pastoral care is done. In other denominations, 'the senior pastor' or 'the minister' fulfils a similar hierarchical role. This may work for a small church (although even then it may not be the best way) but it becomes a major constraint as the church grows numerically.

Anthropologist Robin Dunbar[4] suggests that, because of the size of our neocortex, we can typically only maintain a stable relationship with around one hundred and fifty people. Beyond this number, a group loses its sense of community and belonging. As a result, when we naturally resist losing the sense of 'knowing everyone', we, without knowing it, also resist growing the community.

This applies to both pastor and people. This limits people's ability to pastor effectively. Beyond a certain level, the pastor may feel over-stretched or community discontent sets in. So pastor and people can set a natural plateau for the church. Growth can then only be maintained if leaders find ways to replicate groups of that size (e.g. by church planting) or move on. Beyond this limit, if a church is to grow, it needs a different leadership approach.

To get ahead of the curve, the pastor has to move away from a one-person style of ministry well before the limit is reached. Specifically, this means moving from 'doing the people stuff' to 'making sure the people stuff is done'. It means a clear role change for the overall leader. This does not mean that they cannot continue to do the thing they are most gifted to do (e.g. preach, teach, encourage) but their role becomes better defined and more about the empowerment of others to lead.

Perhaps the biggest change is when all serious pastoral matters no longer get directed through one person. In fact, as a church grows, additional senior roles are needed so that the pastoral/disciple-making oversight is taken on by others, the load is shared and, most important of all, the congregation frees the senior leader from the unspoken but real expectation of omnipresence.

This requires a huge mind-set change on behalf of people and pastor alike, with real costs: the loss of the same sense of community; the loss of the personal attention of the leader; and the feeling that, 'it is not like it used to be'. These things must be spoken of openly, mourned together and moved on from together.

As the curves illustrates, though, perhaps the biggest challenge is that the required changes happen ahead of the visible need. Often the finances are not available to build staff numbers and only become available as growth takes place. There is no immediate problem. Hence the need for faith in the congregation to take the risks involved in making the change early.

Structures

Decision-making structures are a second common obstacle to growth. Churches can be held back by structures that served them well for the size they once were but restrict them now. It is common to see a mid-sized church in a small-sized structure and wondering why things are not working. Equally it is common to see structures that are being used poorly and so constrain growth.

At Lead Academy, we do an exercise which includes asking leaders about their frustrations. The responses are nearly always the same. Those who work as paid members of staff cannot make decisions without having to jump through slow-moving, time-consuming hoops.

The pastor of a growing Baptist church wants to make a small change in the church. He brings it to his fortnightly elders' meeting, a group of busy individuals, and they discuss it but have not had time to think about it beforehand, so defer the decision for two weeks. Two weeks later, they decide to go ahead so then it goes to the church meeting, which is a month away. They too have not been able to think it through so argue it back and forth ... very soon we are three months further on, without any action.

Similar trials can occur in the Anglican Church where the vicar has to pass everything through the PCC (Parochial Church Council), which might meet only bi-monthly. Consultation is vital but too much can get sandbagged in the process.

Both these structures were set up at a particular time in history to correct an imbalance seen elsewhere, because of a particular theological understanding of church or to put structure to a movement that was growing. These kinds of initiatives may help to prevent each generation having to re-invent the wheel but if maintained inflexibly they strangle the development of churches.

Using stewardship as a driver of structure

One church, working through the barriers to change and growth, concluded that a powerful way to rethink about its structure was to examine how well it fitted with its stewardship responsibilities.

The leaders worked out the church's responsibilities in terms of topics like pastoring, teaching, worship and teaching and looked at the extent to which the current structure spoke into the critical areas. Having identified the limitations it then went on to think through how, for each group in the church, this stewardship could best be discharged by allocating it to the right place.

As a result they created a new leadership group which also met to a different pattern to enable it to cover the topics properly and meet the needs of both the different groups in the church and the integration of the development of disciples as a whole.

The key to growth is effective empowerment, with many people able to make decisions. This presents different risks, around control and waste, but these are better risks to run than ossification and can be mitigated by clear purpose. One leader of a large church, challenged with, 'If everyone is empowering everyone else, who is leading the church?', responded that it was not a 'who' but a 'what': ultimately the purpose and vision lead the church and everyone becomes empowered to play their role in it.

These challenges present themselves in every type of church leadership style. It is easy for complexity to abound.

Hierarchical style: Anglican churches represent denominations that have a hierarchical structure of leadership. Incumbents often explain to us the challenges of the 'top-down' structure meeting the 'bottom-up' nature of the local church. This of course includes the impact of diocesan structures, which can impact policies and become particularly important in crisis situations. However, even without these the situation locally can present structural challenges.

The vicar is assumed to be the leader but in reality it is often much less clear-cut. There will be a PCC of elected church members which is often the main decision-making body in the church. Then there will be the churchwardens (the link with the diocese), and possibly a kind of executive, made up of vicar, churchwardens and some readers or PCC reps. Alongside this there will often be task-focused committees as well as any church staff. This structure can become both incredibly cumbersome and confusing for decision making as the church grows.

Most growing churches have a leadership structure that has come about by 'bolting on' new bits instead of radical change. This can lead to these frustrations. The structure does not have the clarity and agility that is needed to separate out roles in a way that matches the day-to-day needs of leading the church, administration, ministry and governance.

Congregational style: Baptist churches are an example of a denomination that represents a 'congregational' style leadership where there is commonly a group of elders and a group of deacons. The elders deal with the spiritual and the deacons the practical. But at the end of the day, all major decisions have to be passed by a church meeting of the congregation. This can become equally restrictive.

The role of the PCC?

One church we visited had a PCC of 36 members. When asked who led the church, everyone declared it was the vicar, despite the fact that all decisions from light bulb changing to new services had come through them. We knew the vicar and his staff felt frustrated by the monthly meeting cycle which achieved so little and served to frustrate him and his other staff members.

Elsewhere the PCC unanimously voted down coffee before the service, the minister reminded them that worship was entirely his responsibility and that for him coffee was part of worship. He asked them to reconsider their vote and challenged the scope of their role.

Originally designed to get away from a hierarchical, top-down structure, the pastor can easily find themselves caught between the elders and the congregation. They can find the pace of decision making and agreeing direction equally ill-matched to the needs of the church and similarly as a church grows the elders and deacons have to take on a less hands-on approach and new leadership structures are needed.

Multi-church style: There has been recent grown in a third style of leadership. This is the multi-church benefice of the Anglican Church and the circuit system of the Methodists. This was a historical pattern laid down in the Methodist Church but the growth in the Anglican Church is due to the shortage of clergy and church decline. Both, however, pose real practical challenges to effective church leadership in the lack of clarity about roles, the definition of churches and the logistics for ministry. As the 'From Anecdote to Evidence'[5] report highlights, this is impacting growth in these situations.

Bishop James Newcome has said that with multi-church benefices in the Church of England there needs to be drastic change in the mind-set and structures of leadership to the extent that, 'the people become priests, the priests become bishops and the bishops become apostles'.[6] That would be a great and liberating change but is costly to bring about.

Whatever the style of leadership it is important that the structure facilitates the healthy direction, function and governance of the church and it is remarkably easy for it to fall out of kilter with the need for agility and growth.

One helpful strategy for growth is to separate out the governance (budget, staff appointments, facilities, guarding the purpose and vision as well as biblical orthodoxy, discipline, etc.) from the team who lead the church on a day-to-day basis. This often means that those who have been hands-on when the church was small need to step back into an oversight role and release leadership to others. It means the congregation must let leaders lead and trust them to do it. If the boundaries of responsibility and accountability are clearly known and written down, then this becomes far more effective.

The challenges here are about people relinquishing power and letting go, something in the main that people do not like to do. It needs skill, courage and resolution to see it through.

Growth requires structures to change. Our structures facilitate the manner in which we meet, express community, execute mission and live out our lives together. They need to change as a church grows. People should never be forced to fit a structure. Structures are there to help the church to be church and for mission to be more effective. They need to respond, just as at some point in many churches house groups were introduced to facilitate fellowship and a deeper sense of community.

Working on better decision making

It can take a process of reflection before the practical challenge of leadership structures come into focus. Phil explained, 'When we were on the Lead Academy learning community, at the second gathering focused on leadership, we sensed that our church was going to be limited by our leadership structure. We knew we needed one that would enable growth, rather than limit it. We talked the whole issue through and decided that having a PCC that met twelve times a year didn't give us enough time to look at vision and strategy. Most of the time in the PCC meetings was spent time talking about finance, staff, youth and children's work, services, events, etc.'

They decided to create a leadership team which met every two weeks and which would focus only on vision and strategy. The PCC then met four times a year and received reports from the leadership team with recommendations and a description of discussion that had taken place. 'We needed to make sure that the members of the PCC did not feel that they were simply there as a rubber stamping exercise. Hopefully we had removed a lot of the pressure of visionary thinking, and were asking the PCC to think about finance and important governance issues, but not needing to think deeply about vision.

'We had already set up a "Business As Usual" meeting which happened every Monday morning, with a small group of people. This meeting looked at the day-to-day running of the church, covering such things as organising social events, rotas, and reflecting on day-to-day issues.' At first, some of the members of the PCC struggled to understand how the whole structure would work so it was agreed to trial it for six months, but it proved to be useful and so has continued.

'Since making the decision, we have taken on a local shop unit which has required a huge amount of work and has needed a team of its own made up from the PCC to oversee the work. If we had stuck with the original PCC structure, we would have overworked people, I am sure, as most of the teams are made up of different people from the PCC. People have valued not having a PCC meeting each month. We certainly need to hone the system, but it seems to be working very well.'

Whenever you make a change to structures, you will invariably upset some people. But change in structure often facilitates real growth in church life. Some churches have developed mid-sized communities, some accountability triplets, others missional communities. Some churches have begun a Fresh Expression, others started church planting, multi-site or multiplied services in their building. Structures change to facilitate life and growth. There is unlikely to be an ideal structure. Nor should there be a permanent one. Organic life needs to remain dynamic.

Buildings

There will be many church leaders who instinctively know that this is one of the common hindrances to ministry and growth. Buildings are a blessing and a curse. Many churches have inherited impractical, old buildings with huge upkeep costs; others have no building and struggle finding a place to rent or meet.

But buildings make a statement and can be highly attractive or profoundly repelling. Churches often grow to about 70-80% of their building capacity and then stop. Actually what happens is a sort of wave effect. One week it is packed and you know you must do something but the next there is space and you think the crisis has abated. This goes on until it settles at a comfortable number, less than full, and nobody really knows why.

There are human dynamics at work in this. Many churches have stopped growing because of this one factor alone. It doesn't matter if a building is large or small, it will at some point restrict your growth. There are countless churches that are praying for growth where it will not happen. They are not prepared to make room for the new people or are under the illusion that they won't make a change until week after week the people cannot get in the building. The problem becomes that the

97

congregation likes the sense of fullness and will usually resist the change until it is too late.

Blessing from adversity

One church in the South of England, that had struggled to see the growth they wanted, found they had serious structural problems with their building. They had to move out and because there was no other large building in the neighbourhood, they decided that the only way forward was to set up a whole number of smaller churches in local communities. A member of the congregation at that time told us, 'We grew faster, released more ministry and had better fellowship than ever before.' This may well not have happened without the crisis.

Similarly, a Baptist church, restricted by its building, had a fire one night (the pastor assured us it wasn't him that started it). Because of the damage, a member of the congregation who owned a car showroom opened it every Sunday morning for the church and they saw a lot of growth in that time.

Timing is important. There is an assumption that because building size inhibits growth, once you deal with the problem the church will grow. But if change is too slow in coming, there is a period of no-growth that the new building may not correct.

When buildings constrain there are many possible ways forward: multiply services, let children meet separately, enlarge or renew buildings, plant a church, etc. In each case though, it is best to choose a way forward and not stick within the confines of the current building.

Focus

As a church grows, it tends to add programmes. These may be created to serve new groups or better deliver the core mission (e.g. an informal service, Messy Church, a friendship club, a food bank, counselling). Yet over time, it is all too easy to become a busy church with lots of increasingly tired people gallantly maintaining a full range of activities with little focus.

Then even individually attractive programmes can end up constraining growth more than enabling it.

Focus is incredibly important if a church is to become what it is destined to be. Running as many programmes as possible and holding a 'good works mentality' is the route to burn-out and ineffectiveness. The cost of focus is stopping some worthwhile activities, and this is why it is hard. Leaders put the decision off so as not to offend. Yet the church slowly grinds to a halt.

At this point it is vital to be clear exactly what your 'why' is and be committed to a 'where'. It is the only way to regain focus. Andy Stanley, pastor of North Point Church, in introducing some teaching on this subject says this: 'The longer a ministry operates, the more complex it becomes. In order to maintain a winning organisation, we must continually face the challenge of narrowing its focus.'[7] In fact, his research showed that churches that focus are more fruitful in the long term than those that don't. There is a balance here, especially as large churches have the capacity to undertake many different activities. The need is to sense where God is moving and align with this.

To grow in the way that God wants your church to grow requires focus and a clear sense of direction. To regain focus requires courageous and resolute change.

Belonging

In business, over the last twenty years, leaders have realised that it can cost many times more to find a new customer than to keep hold of those that they already have and watch the business grow. The same opportunity exists in churches.

Have you ever wondered at how many people come into the church and then soon vanish again? How many times have you heard people say, 'Our back door is wide open'? Often people come through the doors but do not stay.

Let's do some maths. If in a given locality there is a 10% turnover of population every year, a church with fifty members will lose five each year. If they get five new visitors (just to provide equality), they will spot newcomers easily and no doubt be all over them with love. On the other hand, a church of five hundred members, losing fifty each year, may get fifty visitors. The chances are that a good proportion of these will not be spotted and may come and go without being welcomed in a loving and sustained way until they feel part of the community. They get missed not because it is an unfriendly church but because there is no intentional system for embracing people and enabling them to be part of the community.

The majority of both 'churched' and 'non-churched' people are primarily looking for an accepting and loving community. Even though a large church may feel like that to the 'insiders' it won't necessarily be so for newcomers.

This is another common barrier to growth that may need to change. It is not as costly as other things but nevertheless needs committed attention.

Culture

The management guru, Peter Drucker, is credited with saying that, 'Culture eats strategy for breakfast.' This means that your culture sets the pattern for life in the organisation. All strategy needs a culture that is compatible and church culture can often turn away from a missional growth seeking path.

Over time, the culture of the church does change. It can move, for example, from a missional, can do, welcoming community to a consumerist, performance and 'What's in it for me?' mentality. It might start with a passion for mission but with the addition of programmes and people, it ends up prioritising maintenance and 'keeping people happy' becomes the main thing.

Sometimes the need for growth in maturity or numbers requires a wholesale change in values, attitudes and understanding. Culture is perhaps the hardest barrier of all to address. Some analysts even believe it cannot be done in a controlled manner. It carries great risks and takes considerable time. It needs determination and tenacity. Yet it might be vital for growth (see Chapter 16).

In this chapter we have highlighted six of the most common barriers to growth. It takes great wisdom and courage for the leadership of the church to identify those barriers that are really blocking growth and change, early enough to address them before the plateau sets in.

Restless leaders with a clear focus on why the church is there will probably identify them soonest. Then there is the real challenge of confronting the barriers ahead of sclerosis.

Yet it can be done. The early church confronted these sorts of barriers. We see this in the new leaders added to the running of the church,[8] new structures being used to run the church,[9] new nations being addressed[10] and different ways of proclaiming the gospel.[11] God seeks change as the best way to advance his never-changing purpose.

Key point summary
* As a living organism the healthy church community must exhibit growth – growth as captured in Ephesians 4.
* One of the key challenges for leaders is sensing when change is needed. It is often needed when things still seem to be going well. Leaders may feel they are disturbing a 'successful formula' and it can still be time to change.
* There are six common barriers to growth – leadership, structure, buildings, focus, belonging and culture.
* Leaders should expect a growth challenge as they grow, especially towards 120-150 people in the congregation.

- Decision-making structures are an often-overlooked barrier to community growth.
- When churches become programme and management driven they are often in need of renewal to bring back vision and community to the fore.

8 - Get Ready for Change

The start before the start

When change is wholeheartedly accepted by most people, leaders have typically spent a good deal of time in making sure that the ground into which change is sown is ready for planting and that the leadership and the community is in a good position to own the change.

At its fullest this consists of several steps:

- Building a team.
- Identifying and facing up to the concerns that leaders have about change.
- Getting leaders ready to fulfil the leaders' roles.
- Watching out for leaders' bear traps.
- Making sure the community has the capability for the journey.

Inevitably, it is not practically possible to cover all of these before change. Life is rarely that simple. But addressing the main points in this chapter will strengthen the resilience of leaders and community and put in place good foundations for significant change.

Building a team

Frequently, and especially in politics or business, all attention goes on the top person – the Minister, the CEO, the Chief of Staff, the head of the organisation. 'The buck stops' with this person. Organisations and people seem to like this level of accountability. It makes things clear. However, this does not resemble the model of church governance that we see in the early

Christian church in Acts, where there was clearly a team (even if, within the team, there were charismatic individuals).[1]

Governance without team-based leadership, especially in change, is prone to enormous weaknesses. For the organisation, it leaves it dependent on the idiosyncrasies of the individual. We expect this person to have perfect judgment, make all the critical decisions, have all the answers, know what is important and make it happen. This is not realistic, biblical, or indeed the way groups work well. It is certainly not appropriate for most local churches in a Western democracy.

It is not a great place for leaders either. It isolates us at the same time as it demands an impossible brief and a pedestal position that can be a magnet for disruptive personal motivations.

The first task, for any leader coming into a change, is to build, if there is not one already, an effective team to lead the change. This may be the leadership of the church itself. It will need to sponsor any change on behalf of the church. It provides the authority, validation and legitimacy needed for the way forward and can then, if desired, pass the practical leadership of the change to a group that will carry forward implementation.

However, a team is not merely a collection of individuals or an established group where each person looks after their own area. Leaders need to operate effectively as a team, i.e. a group that:

- know and trust each other;
- are open and compassionate with each other and feel accountable for the church and their actions;
- share a picture of the current state and direction of the church (or can work to build one);
- possess a mandate to lead;

> **Team leadership changes the service pattern**
>
> One church that decided to rethink their pattern of weekly services and tailor them better for the delivery of the mission of the church reviewed the need for change in its council meetings where all key leaders were present.
>
> It then decided to set up a separate team with representation from the different groups within the church to decide and lead on the specifics of the change. It mandated this group to make the recommendations and then, once approved, to lead on the implementation. All this made the change to what is a sensitive part of church life a much more widely spread and carefully controlled process – far removed from a decision taken by a single leader.
>
> The value of this could be seen subsequently in this church of capable and often opinionated middle-class people. As the decision was taken and change took place, people much more easily adopted the new and adjusted to it. There was much less fallout than might otherwise have been the case and, where sensitivities were offended, people could see no bad intent and plenty of engagement in the church community so were much less likely to opt out.

- carry close relationships with all different groups within a bigger church;
- jointly make decisions and take actions, not merely react to a single dominant leader; and
- meet regularly and with purpose.

This is groundwork task number one and represents the most powerful lever for change. It compensates for other weaknesses if it is resilient. It can be the motivating force behind effective change. This can be seen in many analyses of successful change initiatives in the commercial world. The most commonly identified critical factor in successful change is what is often called 'senior management commitment', a.k.a. an effective and engaged leadership group. We are sure that this is also true in church. Many subsequent pitfalls can be avoided and difficulties overcome if there is a strong leadership team foundation. Without it, change is precarious.

A focus on building a group like this ahead of anything else increases the likelihood of successful change. It also replicates the pattern through which Jesus launched his ministry.

Identifying leaders' concerns about change

Leaders have concerns about launching into change. Some are specific to the situation. Some are more about change generally. It is valuable to talk about these amongst the leadership group in an open way. This way leaders see that we are not alone in our fears, risks can be identified and a realistic frankness can be cultivated that will help to earth progress in reality.

We asked the Arrow Programme leaders to identify their most important concerns about change (see chart below).2 Most of these concern people and reveal a great deal of foresight over the main challenges that exist in leading change. Often our gut forewarns us of what we are to face. The checklist of their concerns can provide a useful discussion starter for any leadership group. It illustrates the importance leaders place on commitment for real change to happen. The first three of the top four concerns relate to the desire for people in the congregation to fully support the change. Depending on the overall leader and the nature of the situation these concerns manifest themselves differently. Sometimes the practical concern of knowing that there will be some conflict and needing to find the best way to address it, at other times the desire to either encourage those wavering to get behind a new way of doing things or avoid putting people offside.

These concerns were exacerbated by the understanding that positive outcomes from these concerns were outside the control of the leader and sometimes subject to almost irrational or mystical twists and turns. Overall, 30% of the concerns were in this area.

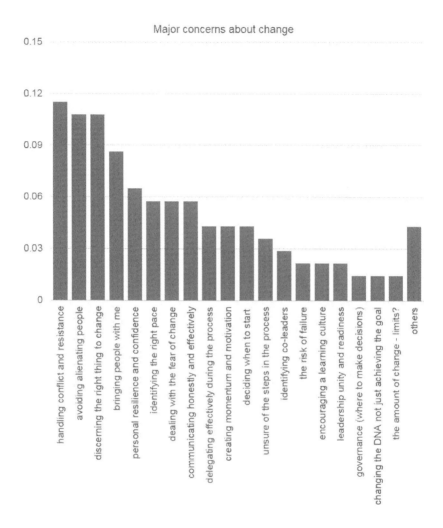

Leaders are right to be concerned about this. A cursory look at the short tenure of football managers, chief executives or those in political positions suggests a close correlation between critical decisions and the departure of leaders. Leaders often become the focus for issues in an organisation, regardless of their personal involvement.

In the US study referred to earlier,[3] most congregations had significant disagreements at some time during the previous five years and these frequently centred on leadership. Leading change will often expose or provoke conflict.

Over 10% of leaders were concerned that they would not discern the right way forward and that they would lead the congregation in the wrong direction. This reveals the self-challenge that Christian leaders need to engage in when contemplating change.

Leaders recognise the isolation that goes with a leadership role and the need to remain resilient and energetic. The need for a good support structure was high on the list.

Similarly, the expression of how to manage people's fear of change was also high on the list and a number of the leaders expressed that this was not only fear among their community but also within themselves as they worried about what they were unleashing.

Leaders' own experiences of change in a church context were quite mixed amongst this group, with an even balance of quite positive and exciting, and poorly conceived and executed changes.

Only at this point in the list do the practical questions about the nature of change itself arise: How fast? How best to communicate? How to get and keep momentum? What steps to follow? These often reflect specific issues from a person's experience or advice that they have been given (exploit the honeymoon period as a new leader, or wait 12 months before you initiate change). Sometimes they reflect specific facts about the church that might influence or constrain progress.

The other factors, that were in each case brought up by no more than one leader, included questions such as whether to move forward in a piecemeal way or as a grand design, handling people who might overly press their view, how much upfront visioning to provide and how much resource change will need.

There were two areas that seem to us to be underestimated by leaders:

1. Few consider failure (rather fewer than will fail ...) and most seem quite confident about the practical governance around a major change (who makes what decisions, how to organise, who to involve, etc). Yet this is an important area to consider if change is to be undertaken well and it is frequently addressed poorly. (See Chapter 12.)
2. There were remarkably few questions about personal skills and specific development needs. It is impossible to know how well-founded is their confidence in their skills (e.g. project management, finance, organisation). Yet this was unlikely to reflect any real depth of experience or training. These are areas where other organisations invest heavily to increase the capability of their leaders.

What do leaders do in change?

Introduction

Leaders play a vital role in change. We shape the direction, timing, character and focus of the church throughout the change. This applies to both those leaders who hold formal positions in the church and those leaders who emerge because of their influence and interactions with others. As we discuss later (Chapter 10), it is helpful to identify leaders from their influence not just by looking at the formal roles in church. A critical skill for the overall leader is the identification and cultivating of leaders from across the church to build a team.

Leaders have a disproportionate impact on the situation – for good or ill – because of the influential position that we occupy. As we discussed in Chapter 5, this includes not just our approach to change but our nature and life in God. Where we come with a considered and calm demeanour we help set a positive tone for the change. If we come into change with our ears open, encouraging even the dissenting voices, the tone is set for an open and involved process of change. Our trust and confidence will set the tone. Trust breeds trust. Confidence breeds calm and the best atmosphere to address issues.

We can breed curiosity to find out what people think, and why, and try to get behind comments and concerns to help people address their issues. We can foster an outward focus on the community and the change rather than an inward focus on the often less important.

Restless leadership

'... the culprit that drives this cycle isn't the
fear of failure so much as it is for many the craving
for success.'
*Daniel Vasella (ex-CEO of Novartis), talking
about the tyranny of successful performance*

One of the important attributes of leadership is to take initiative. There is danger in this. The need to be proactive can lead us to depart from God's leading or damage what is working well. As Dietrich Bonhoeffer wrote, in *Life Together and Prayerbook of the Bible*, 'Those who love their dream of a Christian community more than the Christian community itself become destroyers of that Christian community even though their personal intentions may be ever so honest, earnest, and sacrificial.' Yet leaders need to remain restless for the church.

This is why a combination of questions and confidence are vital attributes. It is why leaders have to be vigilant for growth barriers.

It is easy for groups, communities, organisations and churches to get stuck, even stuck doing what is working. Life can easily become like a drive on a track in the remoter parts of Africa, where one speaker commented, 'Choose your rut well because you will be in it for next 40 miles!' It is healthy for leaders to bring a constant questioning of the issues and opportunities to be addressed.

We get stuck because we do not face challenges and often become disconnected from our environment and others who would bring a natural friction and tension that would naturally promote change.

We get stuck when there is not a good flow of new blood with an external perspective, alternative ideas and the raised eyebrows of seeing something new for the first time. Just as when we don't fix the scratched paintwork in a house in the first six months we soon fail to see the marks.

We get stuck because when the truth hurts we find it easier to change our view rather than alter the reality.

We get stuck because we take criticism as aggression rather than as a starting point for potential improvement.

We get stuck because we dream but we do not organise to act. We want to act boldly when we do not have the resources or energy for anything but small steps and we then can't be bothered to take those small steps.

God's love for us is an expression of continual hope: always progressing, persevering and sanctifying. Leaders need to follow God's lead and seek the truth, always hope, always persist, take the small steps, see obstacles as platforms to reach higher and reach outwards to make connections. Leaders need to be restless or they are not leading. As Gordon Allport, the American psychologist, once said, 'The surest way to lose the truth is to pretend you already possess it.'

The important role of leaders in change

It might seem self-evident that those in leadership have an important role in advancing change. However, consider the popular movements for change in the Arab Spring, the Ukrainian turbulence of 2014, the rise of the Asian economies, and the big shifts in social attitudes that we have seen in the West since World War Two.

What was the contribution of those in formal leadership positions? Often they seemed to try to slow or stop an amorphous force that took on change and swept existing leaders aside to raise up new ones. Only sometimes do we see leaders making a real difference to change – Mikhail Gorbachev, Gandhi, Nelson Mandela.

Sometimes leaders can and do seem to play a valuable role. It is important therefore to understand what leaders specifically can do to lead change effectively. Kouzes and Posner, in their book *The Leadership Challenge*,[4] identified five practices which help leaders to achieve exemplary results with their teams. These five approaches, which they have validated with many thousands of interviews, suggest leaders play their most valuable roles through certain behaviours:

1. Modelling the Way
2. Inspiring a Shared Vision
3. Challenging the Process
4. Enabling Others to Act
5. Encouraging the Heart

Notice how much these speak to us about focusing on others, drawing out their potential and calling forth new actions. There is a lot of helpful material in their analysis that reveals how leaders can most effectively execute their role through periods of both stability and change. Looking at their list, it is also possible to see how it has immediate and enhanced applicability for change.

John Gabarro[5] observed that leaders perform a number of key roles in change:

1. *Good diagnosis and direction*: We can be the orchestrators of a good diagnosis and choice of direction for the community. We do not necessarily need to provide the way forward, have the vision or set the path but we can help make sure that it gets pulled together and that people understand what it is and why it is important. The distinction is an important one. Many people feel that the leader must provide the answers but this is not true. Indeed, sometimes it can be counterproductive; much more often it is questions that are needed. These point people's attention to topics, motives or tasks where they are in the best position to create the answers that are needed. Leaders help to make sure that God's leading is understood and followed.

2. *Creating and maintaining teams*: We are in the best place to make sure that change is a team game. We can build the guiding team for change and help make sure that it is effective in taking the church forward. This role of building and maintaining productive relationships can be critical for times of challenge and disappointment during change.

3. *Boundary setting*: Leaders can also help to ensure that the change is well focused and does or does not involve changing boundaries. Providing permission and leadership for new activities – a youth ministry, a soup kitchen, changes to service

113

patterns. All these sorts of changes need leaders to allow them to put in scope.

4. *Making timely changes*: Left to ourselves we will almost always be too slow in making changes happen. We do not have our eyes on the future and on lead indicators. We will see the opportunities or challenges too late to really capitalise on the situation. As leaders, we play a key role in identifying points for change and then mobilising attention and support to make the change happen quickly enough.

A great way to start the leadership group thinking is to discuss what are the most important roles that leaders need to play in the change and how best to ensure that the group as a whole fulfils this. We may assume that everyone already knows this. Some may, but the discussion will help develop a comprehensive list and emphasise its importance.

Leaders' bear traps

Authority vs omniscience
We are expected to set a different example from the world in leadership. The discussion about who takes the best seats in the kingdom[6] carries important instruction about how the kingdom works and the role of leaders in the church. The Bible offers a withering critique of the top-down, controlling and power-driven leadership that works to its own agenda. It contrasts it with the Jesus' leadership: he holds all the authority, but his example is one of service and the giving of his life for others.

The Bible clearly places all power and authority with God. He is only ever described as the head of the church. Yet he uses his authority carefully and with people's best interests at heart. Despite his omnipotence, God gives free will and he came to set people free.

We see this in the way that Jesus deals with people: his directions to the woman caught in adultery or the rich young ruler[7] both leave them to make their decisions but equally make the way of freedom clear. There are similar teachings in difficult stories such as that of Ananias and Sapphira,[8] where the individual has free choice but deceit is challenged in the strongest terms.

This upside-down attitude has important implications for all followers of Christ but especially leaders:

- The importance of truth as an adjudicator in communications and action.
- Truth and love as drivers of actions.
- Transparency not subterfuge or deceit.
- The goal of change and the means to achieve it must be liberating not enslaving. Power is not used in a coercive fashion.
- People are encouraged to choose and choice is respected but it brings with it consequences and responsibilities.
- Encouragement to love God first and foremost always.
- Overarching authority exists – but it belongs to God not leaders.

There is a necessary humility in leading into change in church that, whilst it does not require everyone to agree, does demand everyone to listen and recognises that no one has a monopoly on truth but all are seeking to hear from God. The first bear pit to avoid is to assume that those who disagree 'are wrong and we need to work out what unreasonable thing is causing this'. Rather, we need to approach different views thinking, 'We may have missed something that we need to consider or take into account.' Our approach to genuine disagreement is a litmus test for authority under God. Proponents and opponents of changes come with good and bad motives and we need to bear this in mind.

A fractured leadership group

A united and committed leadership group is important for successful change. The challenge is when there is not complete agreement about the change. Inevitably not every leader can be committed to a change to the same degree. This is reality. Even leaders take time to get behind something new. The level of commitment can help shape how the change is advanced, prompting suitable caution, testing steps and perhaps pilots or others ways to lead into change more smoothly. It can be managed.

However, some in our core leader group or the wider group of leaders may seek to work actively against the change. In these cases a decision has to be made. If an influential individual or group seeks to block a change (despite engagement and seeking to address their concerns) and the rest of the leadership group are clear that it is the right change to make, then it becomes important to challenge this to prevent it undermining the change. This needs to be done and should be done openly and straightforwardly. If the change is important and the church has been through due process and senses God's leading, then it is essential. Even if the person is a leader within the core group it needs to be addressed.

In some cases this leads to people leaving the church, which is sad but may be essential and, in the end, good for the leaver and for the church. As Gresham's law[9] explains about inflation, 'Bad money drives out good.' The presence of people in leadership pulling in the opposite direction will undermine change unless it is addressed. This needs to be done with dignity but sometimes it needs to be done. Often this person might be in the wrong place or position (stuck in transition) and needs to move on to move forward.

Equally it can be important to attract someone to the core group to help bring about the change – and sensing when this is the case and making suitable steps to do this either directly or indirectly can be an important part of succeeding with a change.

Community capability

Sometimes it is not just leadership capability but community capability that is important for moving forward in change. Examining the position of the community can often highlight important steps that can be taken before change and significantly enhance the probability of success. Sometimes these pre-change activities can become a change in themselves.

The most important areas to consider in a church setting are these:

1. Capability

Capability includes skills of various different types depending on the nature of the change. If we are adding to the number of church gatherings and modernising the musical support this might need people with appropriate musical skills, sound desk skills and hospitality skills (refreshments, guides, administrators). If it is a major building project it almost certainly needs some project management and financial skills and availability.

However, in addition to this, people need to be resilient and ready to face change with the shocks, emotions and potential conflict that this might cause. It is worth building resilience ahead of change to make sure that people have the personal skills to cope more effectively.

Resilience is developed by many different things. At its foundation is being able to help people find meaning as things change, see the context for what is happening and build a story to explain what happens. This means helping people to relate change to the motivations and values of the congregation.

We can explain what happens as we experience change, encourage reflection on change situations in the Bible, make sure people are well anchored in relationships or groups in which they are able to be open and honest and help them to understand the common nature of their feelings as things unfold. All these things build capability.

There is no magic system for assessing capability. It is a matter of judgment but perhaps some reflection on the following questions might help:

- Have people in the church experienced a lot of change over the last ten years?
- In interactions with people, do they get fearful or agitated when change is taking place in their lives or is discussed in the group?
- Walk through potential areas of change and consider: what technical skills will be needed at each stage of launching, implementation and running something new? Are any a huge stretch that needs prayer?
- Will the change involve lots of people and groups? Are each well understood?
- How much of a desire is there to move on, both in terms of the number of people who want it and the depth of feeling for it?

2. Group engagement and relationships

If a group is not well integrated one with another, and remains distant from those seeking to move forward, then the lack of engagement can make the church weak overall. People who do not feel part of a community will not find it easy to appreciate leaders who seek change or the value of the end goal; nor will they be willing to endure the discomfort of the 'neutral zone' during the change. It is highly likely that they will check out.

If we sense that people do not have a reasonable level of commitment to the group then it may necessary to start activities that help build a sense of unity and affinity. Some analysts see 'spiritual and relational vitality'[10] as a vital foundation for any major change and these are certainly important for underpinning other changes.

3. Encouragement and support

Sometimes, particularly where capabilities are lacking, it is possible for leaders to put in place support structures that can mitigate or resolve the challenge. This could be training and educational support (e.g. exploring how people will feel as they go through a change), special meetings (e.g. for prayer and counselling, for managing aspects of the change), prayer or coaching partnerships, or encouragement from another church or group in the church.

Sometimes it makes sense to look at the church calendar and make sure that there are gatherings that allow support to be given easily to help people through a tough time. These might be related to the change, or fun times that stimulate fellowship and get people together in an easy setting.

Trialling ways to encourage people before the change can be useful because these can then often be carried on through the change itself and, having been established beforehand, they can prove to be effective in meeting people's needs.

4. Focus

Where people need to make a major change in their life, it requires focus. Unless a change is high enough on the church agenda and it gets real leadership it is unlikely to happen. The new service format won't stick and will gradually either drift back or lose people to other services. The prayer commitment will fade or special events will get farther and farther apart in the diary. The new leadership structure will get bypassed.

All such things happen because the change is not high enough on the leadership and church agenda. If we want change then we must give it the priority that it needs.

Key point summary

- A key starting point for change is to make sure that there is an effective leadership team with a readiness for change.
- Leaders can then face up to their concerns about change together. Leaders have a wide range of concerns about change. Important amongst these are concerns about: conflict, generating commitment, making the right change in the best way, and personal resilience.
- Leaders play important roles in change. This starts with a restlessness to trigger timely change and continues with their significance in providing clarity to the change, maintaining enthusiasm and team working, and modelling the change.
- Community capability is also important. This is not only about skills but also relationships, engagement and support structures.

9 - Godly Dissatisfaction

The change journey invariably starts with some sort of dissatisfaction: a reframing that makes the current position unacceptable and provides the energy to get to a better place. To begin requires:

- the creation of dissatisfaction that prompts change;
- dissatisfaction that is a personally felt pain;
- good reasons to change mind; and maybe
- a mandate for change.

The trigger for change

In church situations the genesis of change tends to be much more opaque than in commercial organisations. In business there will often be a clear driver. It can take many forms. It might be an adverse trend in a key management metric (like margins, customer satisfaction, employee turnover). It might be a significant environmental event (a new entrant to the market, regulatory intervention, a move in the exchange rate) or a local issue (loss of a major customer, defection of a group of managers). It may be imposed from above (new targets, a merger, a new organisation) and sometimes it will be generated by a new leader or team, or a review process that identifies a need to alter things that have hitherto been ignored.

In churches, there are these triggers. But in listening to leaders talk about their situations the more frequent reasons are more subtle. They are shifts in the environment (e.g. local demographics, a new housing estate) or experiences of decline, change or growth in membership. Often they are associated with the arrival of a new leader with a fresh pair of eyes and new ideas about how to fulfil the ministry of the church locally.

This makes it more difficult to identify when change is needed and more difficult to decide if it is a big change (rather than an incremental one) for a community. All this makes careful diagnosis of the current situation a frequent topic of conversation between leaders when they share their church concerns with each other.

When we think about change we rapidly focus on the end. It is the bit that excites us. There is a natural tendency to jump over the journey to focus on the solution. Yet the journey is just as important. In approaching change we need to remember that as Dorothy L. Sayers said, 'Life is not a problem to be solved but a work to be made.'[1]

It is, as a lot of creative works are, a journey started by dissatisfaction.

Change starts with dissatisfaction

Big D

A church had a difficult geographic situation. Its parish was split by a large park through which no road passed. One side of the park was an aspirational new estate of modern houses and the other a much older and less affluent area. The church had three centres – one in each side and one in the middle of the park. Two of these had a natural community pool to drawn on but the 'mother building', the oldest one, sat in the park and had no clear role or catchment.

A new minister was appointed to the parish just as financial considerations were forcing reductions in the numbers of paid staff. It did not take him long to appreciate the difficult position of the structure of the parish and the buildings and the need to address this. He began to talk about a new direction and how to move forward. However, the solution he offered met with immense hostility from one of the centres that saw it as an attack on its identity and mission. The solution created friction with both the congregation and staff at this centre. Similarly, it was not welcomed by the centre on the other side of the parish.

The resulting conflict almost destroyed the incoming minister, the ministry of two of the three centres and the outreach within the parish. It has taken over twenty years for a recovery in the ministry and identity of the church community.

This true story illustrates perhaps the most important point about change and inner transition. Every transition must begin with an ending. We have to feel the pain of staying put before we will move forward. People have to leave before they start a journey. If a vision is offered before people are ready to move, then, at best, it is ignored and, at worst, they attack it and the bearer of the vision.

It is easy as a leader, especially one who is new into a situation, to jump straight to possibilities for the future, to a vision of the future that answers challenges that seem self-evident but in reality are not clear to any of the other involved people. It is equally easy for leaders' thinking to be done in private. We may then forget that the PCC or the church has not been through this process and needs to start with the issues not the solution.

The starting point for change is a clear understanding of why things need to change. These reasons need to be ones that are important to the people of the church.

Change comes out of a crisis, a burning platform, or a compelling reason to move. One Harvard academic described it like this: 'If you want change you need dissatisfaction and the bigger the change that you want the greater the dissatisfaction that is required. Big Change needs Big D.' Why do we need this? It is to do with the dynamics of change that were explained in

Chapter 4. We prefer not to change our expectations. To change them creates loss. We find it easiest to change our perception of reality rather than reality itself. So to change we need us to feel enough 'pain' now to make it worthwhile facing the discomfort of moving to the neutral zone.

Pain often strikes people as a negative feeling but this is a gross oversimplification. The reason that lepers damage their bodies so much is not so much direct damage by the leprosy but self-damage because of the loss of nerve feeling and the absence of pain. Pain is a powerful signal of the need to do something. It can be a valuable signal of the need to move, just as when your hand gets too close to a heat source that will burn the skin, or muscles ache indicating that they need rest.

As leaders we need to become effective at communicating this sense of discomfort. However, there are important features to this dissatisfaction:

- The need to move must be felt by all relevant groups or individuals (or at least build up to this, so that it is felt by all). It is no good if only a few people feel the need but others are fine with things as they are. This will only create friction, division and obstacles. Leaders who surround themselves with just a few trusted confidants will not build this dissatisfaction. The breadth of dissatisfaction needs to be wide enough for it to be recognised in all pockets of the church.
- It will be multifaceted. A single motivation would imply that everyone thinks in the same way. This is rarely the case especially in a body as diverse as church. It is probably a composite set of factors that together make people feel that things need to change.
- These factors can be positive (the motives for capitalising on a changed future) and negative (we must avoid this happening or get rid of this issue). There is pain that

comes from missing out as well as from current problems. Both motivations are valuable because different people respond more sensitively to one or the other

---

Selling the need for change – problem meet solution

We have been involved in the change process in a large church that is planning to plant another congregation. The leaders have done a superb job in communicating the nature of the change but they have concentrated on the excitement of all the possibilities this affords. All this is really good but they have majored on the solution but few have really grasped that there is a problem that needs addressing.

The problem is certainly there. The current services are over-full, the church sees a core part of their mission as introducing people to Jesus and there is a neighbourhood where some of the congregation live where there is both need and opportunity for the gospel.

The change would have been made much easier if people's attention had been directed to the 'problem' and they had bought into it. They themselves would have come up with the solution as quickly as the leaders. The painful 'why' becomes key to the necessity for change. The church would realise that they cannot do what they know they are called to if the present conditions remain as they are.

- It demands change now not later. There needs to be a sense of it must happen now otherwise it can be postponed and in all likelihood will be postponed.
- Finally and most importantly, it is a reflection of what is on God's heart for the community or what he is doing in the area. It is the wind of the Spirit that moves the church. It is not the destination to which the wind blows but a direction that moves away from where the church is standing at the moment.

In our experience leaders often start in the wrong place – much closer to a solution or a goal, rather than with the motives for change. Many times even when they start at this point they do not stay long enough. A broad swathe of people, feeling

125

uncomfortable for long enough, is needed to generate a commitment to move forward. Ironically, the more empathetic the leader, the more difficult it can be. The rescue instinct doesn't like people feeling dissatisfied. Yet people have to feel enough pain to disengage from the present before they can embrace the future. It is really important to remember this.

Starting with these dissatisfiers enables people to leave the right things behind. It helps sequence and shape the future. It helps explain what people feel they are losing.

Pain needs to be felt personally

Have you ever wondered how people finally decide to change a habit – lose weight, get fit, start to recycle, give up smoking or adopt similar behaviour changes? People can have all the rational reasons that are needed to make the case for change but not do anything about it. The facts needed to make a good decision are not enough to provoke a decision to make the change. We can absorb the argument and information and still not feel the pain to change. Sometimes it can be that we are generous to ourselves and give ourselves temporary reasons for not making the change. At other times we condemn ourselves for our lack of action and develop a form of learned helplessness that ironically makes it more difficult for us to take action based on what we know.

It can often take several years without any behaviour change occurring. Then sometimes, seemingly out of nowhere, a sudden change of heart will happen and we stop or start an activity virtually overnight.

What actually triggers the change when it finally comes? Why, all of a sudden, do we come to the decision to change? What are we thinking? Why are the reasons good enough then? The process is, as John Kotter describes it: 'see-feel-change' rather than 'analyse-think-change'.

126

It seems to require a trigger that creates cognitive dissonance (a.k.a. pain) to change our behaviour. This pain is often a clash between our sense of identity and values (what is right and good and where we sit versus these) and our current behaviour. The trigger strips away an internal narrative or rationale that has muted the mismatch between behaviour and self-image.

For the change to take place we have to feel the dissatisfaction of the current situation personally and be unable to rationalise it away. This produces tremendous hurt. It is this hurt that triggers the change. It is why change sometimes begins with a 'moment of truth', an event that brings powerfully to life why things need to change, just as when Rosa Parks refused to move from her seat on the bus.

In church, this might be when a family arrives at a service with several young children and there is no provision for them to participate easily, or when the loss of many previously enthusiastic teenagers shows the need for a more youth accessible service.

The importance of personal challenge

In one study of lifestyle changes[2] (something that is perhaps quite a good proxy for spiritual changes) this trigger event was some kind of comment or challenge from a respected person. This was a close friend or someone whose opinion was valued, a 'significant other'. This personal challenge occurred in 75% of all changes. It might have been a question that challenged the gap between behaviour and espoused values or an off-the-cuff comment in a conversation. People felt this personally. They could not hide in the crowd but recognised that it applied to them. The same is often needed in church.

This is tough. We don't like to admit that we are not OK. We have this natural self-defence mechanism to keep us healthy, especially in the face of tough circumstances. This is why it requires a powerful spiritual work for us to repent. Instinctively recognising this, we are shy of really challenging people when we see the need to change. Yet leaders need to develop this capacity both for themselves and others. One of the greatest services that leaders can provide to others is to help them to see a truth, sometimes an uncomfortable one, in a way that influences their feelings.

The triumph of identity over preferences

One church leader shared with us a marvellous and heart-warming story about the value of dissatisfaction in overcoming even personal likes and dislikes with the way corporate worship is conducted.

The minister had been brought into this church to develop its outreach into the city suburbs in which the church building was located. It had an elderly but mature congregation with a real heart for God but a traditional style and approach to corporate worship.

After several months in which the stirrings of change in new families, activities and thinking were disturbing the pattern of what had been well established, the minister sensed the reticence of the leaders who had brought him into the church and felt the need to talk things through with them.

In a reflective and emotional set of conversations they expressed their discomfort with some of the 'modernising' actions that had been introduced and that were clearly the forerunners of more change.

However, their feelings were voiced by one of the most respected members of the church when he said to the minister that indeed many of these things were not to their liking but that they felt God's calling to move the church on and that even if they seemed a little reticent they were 100% behind what he was doing and wanted him to press on with their full support.

Their understanding and identification with God's work overpowered any personal discomfort.

Dialogue with people, even opponents of the change, is critical. This can be talking individually with key people and groups. It can be explaining the reasoning and direction, sharing the challenging questions that the change addresses, and chatting through the issues.

It needs open disagreement that is not conducted disagreeably. The issues need to be on one side of the table and we need to be sitting together on the other. Where possible we need to maintain the relationship. However, this is not all that is needed to move forward:

- We must feel personally that we are able to change successfully. If we don't we tend not to try.
- We must understand the rationale for changing. Our minds must be satisfied.
- It helps us if it is convenient. This may seem odd but it is important that we see now as a good time to make the change.

This emphasises the importance of how the need for change is communicated. We tend to spend much of our time on autopilot and the busy routine of daily living reinforces this. Our everyday habits are a way of conserving energy. They save us having to make decisions about the huge number of often less important items that we do each day. This enables us to focus on the more important things.

It is therefore important that, at the right time, when a challenge is being made or a change signalled, that it is done in such a way as to catch people's attention. Important because, as William Bridges remarks, 'More often than not, it turns out that the ending is not some external situation but an attitude or an assumption or a self-image.' The timing, medium and method is as important as the message itself.

In church, it is why a special event, building or meeting can be such a useful tool. The new context helps us all to disengage the autopilot, especially if we are encouraged to lean forward and participate rather than lean back and only listen. Special prayer meetings or well-orchestrated church gatherings at a different venue are useful. The different environment signals the need to pay attention.

Reasons to change our minds

'Faced with the choice between changing
one's mind and proving that there is no need to do
so, almost everybody gets busy on the proof.'

J. K. Galbraith

What then can we say and do to help people's thinking develop along new lines. Often our own ideas run along the same lines for quite a long time. They might develop but essentially they stay on the same track until a point is reached at which we start to think differently. How can leaders provoke this change of heart and mind?

We've talked about the importance of pain or crisis. There are ways for leaders to facilitate rethinking and generate support for new actions or behaviours. Leaders can enable the congregation to pay attention to the area where change is needed and then provide the opportunity and information for people to change their minds. How?

Howard Gardner, in his book *Changing Minds*,[3] identifies six reasons why people change their minds based on his research and observations over many years. These six represent helpful approaches for leader interventions:

- *Reason*: People, especially educated people, expect to be able to understand and examine the rationale or logic for a decision and then decide what they think. The presentation and discussion of the logic is an important lever in changing views. We have seen analytical justifications for changes in church (e.g. for changes in service patterns) but more often reason is used in a rhetorical fashion. In secular organisations, we have presented 'case for change' documents to explain the reasoning that supports a new direction. In one organisation, the importance of this document was evident in the fact that it got to version sixteen before it was finalised and it represented input from a wide group of decision makers.

- *Research*: Some groups will want to understand and examine a topic in more detail, either examining the evidence for something or observing or testing the idea to assess its validity. Pilots, surveys, the experience of other churches, formal review processes that shape development – all these can help people to see new possibilities. Inviting people to experience something new elsewhere can often quickly reshape thinking.
- *Resonance*: People come to any issue with their own values, stories and perspectives. Presenting a change in ways that pull out the resonance with past history, heritage and culture is another way for us to help people alter their views. The use of stories and case examples can often be a great way of exploiting this lever for change. Relating the history or timeline of a community and linking the change into this can be a powerful way to support change.
- *Re-presentations*: We all know that sometimes it takes an idea to be seen in a different way – through a picture, a story, an alternative argument or some other presentation of the same concept – before we get it. We each have different triggers and describing the change in different ways helps everyone to catch on. Discussion

often unlocks these different ways of looking at things and is very important. Similarly, multiple presentations of the ideas – in formal talks, through booklets or newsletters and through the use of relevant Bible passages and analogies can all help. In other situations, tools like 'Day in the life of ...' re-enactments or reflection on images or pictures can help to unlock and develop ideas, depending on the nature of the change (see Chapter 12).

- *Resources*: Sometimes for people to believe in a change they may need to know enough about the scale of resources (people, money, time, etc.) that will be put behind it. This can be important information to present when a change is being discussed to enable people to believe in the possibility of success.

- *Real events*: Sometimes a critical event will change people's mind on a topic or on the value of an idea. Events can be harnessed by leaders.

People do change their minds

Visiting a church in the North of England where they had done a magnificent reordering of the interior of the main sanctuary, the woodwork looked stunning and comfortable new chairs had replaced the pews.

Whilst waiting for my host we spoke to a lady and commented on how nice the building was. Her reply surprised us, 'Yes. Well, I totally disagreed with the changes, I was upset. Not only that but I was aggressive in my opposition but eventually I could see that my wishes were not being granted and reluctantly watched them destroy the church I had known for a long time.'

Asked what she thought now. 'Absolutely fantastic,' she replied, 'it has given the church a whole new lease of life.'

Howard Gardner also discusses a seventh factor, resistance. This takes us to some of the issues that we discuss in

Chapter 14 on conflict. Even using all his suggested approaches, there are always likely to be some who will not alter their views. All we can do is minimise this by our overall approach to change.

What is sure, though, is that interaction is needed. Most people do not change their mind in the face of the kind of intellectual assault that you often see portrayed in an episode of *West Wing*. They need to contribute to a dialogue and shape the outcome. Dialogue helps people to move from mere talk about challenging issues to engagement in shaping the way forward. It helps to free resistance.

A mandate for incoming leaders

Often, leaders embark on change when they are coming into a new situation. In itself it can enable leaders to bring dissatisfaction to the surface and form a mandate for change. Whenever a leader moves into a new role it can be an important opportunity to start to shape expectations and crystallise the dissatisfaction needed for change to proceed.

This could be a different role in the church, moving to lead or participate in a new church community, or where there has been a marked shift in conditions impacting the church which has led to sharp changes in congregational expectations of the leaders (e.g. numbers of staff, monetary position, building closures). Sometimes the opportunity is clear, sometimes less so, but moves can often help to prepare the ground for subsequent change.

Where leaders come into communities from outside (as in many of the established churches) there is often a selection process which provides the opportunity to understand more about the situation and expectations of the church. This in turn offers a point for the leader to shape expectations.

Sometimes it is obvious. All too frequently the parish representatives in an Anglican church will, during the interview, ask questions about the candidate's vision for the church. We are

133

not sure what answer they would want to hear to this question. It quite rightly strikes many leaders as an odd question because it presupposes that on our own we carry a 'vision' around in our heads that we will apply to a new church without any real assessment of the current position, needs and people. This is unlikely to be a well-founded vision, even if informed by the parish profile.

Nonetheless, the process of taking up a new role is a great opportunity to find out what the current issues, expectations and values are that the church will bring to new leaders. It provides an opportunity to shape expectations and make the mandate for the leader clearer. This can be useful in preparing the ground where an incoming leader senses that there is going to be the need for significant change that is not yet well understood or identified. Questions directed into the challenges or issues highlighted, peeling back the rationale for circumstances to hunt for root causes, and demonstrating a preparedness to talk openly about difficult topics – all these make it clear that a leader will tackle the issues.

It is always helpful to negotiate a 'mandate' that aligns expectations between the incoming and incumbent leaders. A public alignment can help to ensure that the kind of misunderstandings that feed conflict and obstacles are avoided from the start. The discussion can also help leaders to match their skills and passions with the church. Leaders bring different skills, thickness of skins, gifts, passions and strengths. It is important to play from these strengths and match them to the needs of the congregation and situation. Even beyond the obvious factors (e.g. rural vs urban, size of staff, mission), some people are much better where the style of leadership is collaborative, others where the expectation is of more individual decision making. Some are much more comfortable with a major upheaval in all aspects of church, which is likely to produce greater conflict. Others will prefer to be building on strong foundations. Some will expect to troubleshoot and move on others to dig in for a long stretch. Getting a sense of the expectations of the existing church leaders when going through selection is helpful for starting in the best place and building an agreed mandate.

One topic that has come up frequently in discussions with leaders is the question of whether or not an incoming minister should change things immediately or wait. Leaders receive contradictory advice from senior staff and experienced leaders. This indicates that there is no universally right answer. The Harvard academic, John Gabarro, many years ago studied how incoming Chief Executives operated when they took over in a new company.[4] The results were quite fascinating and support both the value of immediate action and the need for caution. In cases where they started and the business prospered over their tenure the average number of organisational changes that they implemented over their first two years was as follows:

0 - 6 months	6-7
6 - 12 months	3
12 -18 months	7-8
18 - 24 months	4-5

So there were more in the second year than the first and a lull after the first wave of changes. In summary, they addressed the obvious changes that were needed as soon as was practicable and then waited to see how these worked. However, they were not afraid to change things again once they understood better the situation and the impact of the first set of changes. In short, they acted immediately and they waited.

Working with the dynamics of change means starting with an ending and beginning with a clear rationale for not continuing with what has been done so far. If we are serious about a major change we will linger longer and more broadly on this dissatisfaction than we have historically done. In this way we can help people to embrace change.

Key point summary

- Transition begins with a real, shared dissatisfaction with the current state of things. Big change needs big dissatisfaction.
- Triggers for individuals in church to change need to be felt personally. This means that pain will precede effective change and people often need to be challenged.
- We change our minds because:
  - There is a good rationale to do so.
  - We understand the evidence base (often personally).
  - The change resonates with our values and history.
  - We hear and see things presented in different ways.
  - We see ways in which change can be achieved.
  - A critical event flips our thinking.
- Incoming leaders should seek to establish a mandate for change.

10 - Identify People and Roles

Sometimes people seem to behave almost as a caricature of the job or context that you meet them in. It can be quite amusing if someone is playing out the dynamic leader or the excellent host with the inclusion of all the right grand gestures. Yet in reality we all play these sorts of roles, knowingly or unknowingly.

It is easy to see this. The answer to the question, 'Who am I?' will almost always instinctively involve a role. Our roles are close to our identity. They define how we relate to others and in doing so who we are. This is one reason that major life shifts like starting work, beginning a family, or experiencing redundancy, a new job or retirement are so significant. In some way they redefine us.

This chapter highlights the roles that we play in an organisation and those that we play when we are involved in a change. In particular, we highlight the four most important roles in change, roles that if we are leading change, we need to consider carefully.

We all play roles

In any, especially more complex, groups there are roles that people start to fulfil naturally and often unhelpfully. This is the origin of the insight that runs through much systems-based thinking and it is beautifully described by analysts like Barry Oshry.[1] He outlines roles that people play in any organisation. Perhaps the most important of these are the 'tops, middles and bottoms'. The titles are entirely descriptive of who and what he means. In a church context these might represent, for instance:

Tops – ministers and staff team, maybe church council

Middles – maybe council, home group or volunteer leaders

Bottoms – everyone else

The roles can be self-ascribed. No one needs to define them although typically they are defined by the way that the organisation or group works. People pick up the cues for what role they are playing subconsciously and quickly. The impact is profound and can be uncovered by talking with people in each group about the way that they see the world and what they do.

The 'tops' will explain the complexity of their role and the responsibility that they have and must take care of. They will feel the burden of leadership and the need for direction and decision. They lean forward to move the group forward.

The 'middles' will describe themselves being pulled in two directions (by the 'tops' and the 'bottoms'). They are conflicted by, on the one hand, feeling the need to make things happen that fit with the vision, the policies or the requirements of day-to-day operations and, on the other hand, experiencing the practical challenges, the exceptions to the rule and the difficulties of doing this. They will see themselves as sitting in the gap between priorities and the reality on the ground.

The 'bottoms' feel a degree of invisibility and vulnerability. They see themselves as without influence, except as a group and as the targets or recipients of what happens, with little individual responsibility. They lean back and see others as responsible ... especially the 'tops'.

Oshry paints a powerful picture of the pattern of life in an organisation. In his workshops he enables people to experience this pattern of life for themselves. It is a dance between different interdependent partners with all the friction that this involves. It brings with it significant dangers in churches just as in other organisations, especially during change when it can quickly fuel the idea that change is 'being done to us again'. People fall into these roles often without thinking for a number of reasons:

- Much of what we say on a day-to-day basis as we interact is dependent on what each of us is doing (i.e. our role in the situation). In this way it is really a discussion, as Oshry describes it, from context to context. However, we normally interpret it personally and it shapes how we see ourselves and others.

- We don't like mysteries. The essence of a good story is the way it generates questions in our minds that then, as the story unfolds, we are able to answer. This gap between question and answer is what keeps our attention. Infilling the answer is part of the enjoyment. Unfortunately, as a result, when we interact with others from one context to another and do not give all the background, perspective and reasoning, then the other person fills in the details and provides their own answers. We end up then 'playing a role' without understanding how others see us and the situation.

- There is a security in having a clear reasoning and story about why we behave as we do and why we do and say what we do. This quickly defaults to reasoning and stories that end up being 'us and them' in nature.

The Joshua Group – bringing structure to consultation

Travel back in time to an event described in the book of Numbers. The children of Israel are making good progress across the desert to the promised land. This is a journey of only a few weeks. But there is a big change coming as they cross over the Jordan into the land that God has promised them, so Moses sends out twelve spies to check out the land. When they return (Numbers 13), they give a full report to Moses and the assembled people.

They speak of the giants as well as the fruit but they give much more emphasis to the former than the latter. Ten provide a bad report,

---

impressing on the people that they could not possibly overcome the powerful enemy they would face. The people are distraught and turn against Moses. Yet Caleb and Joshua encourage them that the land is plentiful and if God is with them they can overcome any enemy. So what do they do? They don't go in but then spend forty years wandering around the desert.

Who was to blame for this? Moses? He had faith to go in. The people? They only had the report to go on. It was the ten spies. By the way they reported, they set out to dissuade the people from entering into their inheritance. So who were these people? They were leaders in their tribes. In other words, a group of middle managers actually determined whether or not the change would happen. There is an important lesson here.

If on Sunday the leaders announce to the whole church that they have decided to scrap the morning service and only meet in the evening, there might be a deep intake of breath and some murmuring but not much else. Come Tuesday home group, everything is different and out it comes. One of leaders is put on the spot and admits he had been in on the conversations but had been won over by the reasons put forward and he explains why. The majority may then still go along, backing his judgment as they have learnt to trust him.

In another group the leader expresses her ongoing misgivings in no uncertain terms. By the end of the evening the 'anti' brigade are even more resolute and vocal, pulling others off the fence. Who really has the influence? The senior leaders? The congregation? In fact, it is those in the middle. So, a wise senior leader will mobilise this middle group as a sounding board and a place to hone new ideas, to smooth a path to successful change or bring the whole thing to a halt.

The group can be useful, especially in larger churches. In one church, they were called the Joshua group and later the wider leadership group. It was made up of everyone who led something or influenced others. They met once a month for an evening, initially crowding into a large living room, sitting on the floor, drinking coffee and eating cake. So, people wanted to be at these meetings because they could be heard, they were the first to hear of new ideas on direction and because it was by invitation only. Every six months, there was a day away with an even broader group of people to bring even more people up to speed.

This Joshua group provided an effective way to bring in changes, large and small, in a way that bred trust and helped build consensus. It was not a decision-making body. The leaders led, even if they got it wrong. It was a sounding board comprising the people of influence who would not be on the PCC or church council. The evenings comprised an important and fun social time at the start and prayer plus two components:

1. Listening: asking questions. How are we doing? What is the word on the street? Where are the issues we should be addressing? Here was the best feedback you could ever hope to get, from people near the coalface of church life. They were picking up the stuff that otherwise leaders never hear until it is far too late.
2. Sharing: capturing new thoughts. This was the best place for the leaders to sound out early ideas for change, get a response and talk through the issues that would be encountered, letting them grasp how this related to the 'why' of the church. Often there would be creative disagreement which would end up shaping the end result of the new ideas.

Everyone felt consulted. There were two rules that helped the group function:

Openness. If you disagree with something, you need to share it there, not behind people's backs afterwards. Your view will be heard even if it is not eventually acted upon.

Loyalty. Everyone has a say and all understand that it is unlikely there everyone will agree. However, if the group decides to go forward, everyone will speak well of it to the people they lead.

These context-driven behaviours carry into all types of groups including churches and set a backdrop for change. Understanding where people see themselves in church can be valuable for understanding how they may respond to a change and how as leaders we might best encourage them to participate effectively.

The key roles in a change

The four roles

In change situations, there are also roles that people tend to adopt either because they are given them or just because of who they are and where they sit in the community. One of our tasks as the leadership team is to identify who fulfils these roles and address them effectively. The three most important roles exist in all changes and typically the fourth will also be there.

Leaders

Most people assume that leaders are the people who fill the formal managerial roles in any organisation but this is certainly not always the case and especially so in churches.

Leaders can be recognised by their influence and the fact that others look to them for leadership on issues or activities. They will be people who are consulted 'to see what they think about ...'; they may well lead or organise aspects of church life and if they are effective these will prosper in the life of the church. They are people who are prepared to take on responsibility. They are able and do make decisions that will typically get actioned.

Many will be sitting in the obvious chairs: the church governing body, the ministry team, the key leadership positions. There will almost certainly be some elsewhere. Some of these leaders will often have more influence than those in the formal positions.

A mistake that can be made is to confuse administration or day-to-day activity and management with leadership. They are not the same thing. Leaders will influence opinions and engage

142

with others to share their views. Yet many occupying the formal positions will not do this (e.g. many on the typical Parochial Church Council).

Hopefully within the leadership team of the church there will be the most important influencers in the church, people to whom others look for guidance and direction. This is the bedrock of success as described in Chapter 8. However, especially in larger churches, there will be other important leaders whose support is important to sustain to cascade the backing for change throughout the whole of the relevant community.

It may not always be easy to identify the leaders before the change. A more participative approach, coming into change, allows the leadership team to identify key influencers. The leadership team need to look for them. This also enables us to gauge our own commitment to a change. This can sometimes be difficult, especially when a strong leader is advocating it. To uncover real levels of commitment in the team and the nature of any concerns or reservations, the initiator needs to set the right tone for discussion and be genuinely interested in hearing any issues. Advocacy should invite questions and concerns. Dominating the airwaves does not dominate the hearts.

For change to really take place, we must pass the baton of enthusiasm from person to person, in the leadership group and then across the church. As leaders, we need to appreciate the importance of our role:

- To shape change so that people own it before God.
- To understand and honestly support the key components of the change.
- To engage people and discuss the change with them, encouraging them to support it but encouraging questioning to elicit honest opinions.

143

- To feedback, where practical issues arise or changes need to be made.
- To challenge people's opinions and behaviour where they fall short of God's standards.
- To reflect on progress and pray for the change.

The paradox about this list is that sometimes leaders will not be identified until they start to practise these things and by behaving in this way they become leaders.

Participants – sometimes everyone
The second important role that people play in change is to participate in it. Leaders by definition are also participants but the real value of calling out this role is to identify the different groups or constituencies that are going to participate in the change ... and to do so before the change begins.

Even in smaller churches there are different participant groups. These might be groups of close friends, groups built around an activity (e.g. worship, choir, hobby clubs, youth ministry, cell groups, children's classes), a different area or a different service. Leaders need to work at the level of individuals and smaller groups not just with church en bloc. Otherwise we will fail to engage with their concerns, issues and understanding. The wider the change, the more numerous the different groups. This is why typically the bigger the change the broader the leadership group that needs to be engaged and mobilised – because it needs to cover a lot of people.

Understanding the different views and perspectives is important in making sure that:

- Motivations to change and the losses that people feel are understood.
- People and significant events or experiences can be marked.

144

- The importance and impact of the change on people is known and can be articulated.

Change agents

In every change, people respond with differing degrees of enthusiasm and commitment. Some are slow to engage, others much faster. Some grab it and run, being prepared to take on new tasks or responsibilities and make parts of the change happen. These people are playing the role of agents of change, those who will make it happen. They have energy for the change and are ready to help lead parts of the change, perhaps using relevant skills or because of the position that they are have within the body.

It is not necessarily possible to identify these people in advance. However, where there is a period of exploring and testing the best way forward then change agents will often emerge and can be co-opted to help make things happen.

There are some people who may put themselves forward but who are best discouraged. Their desire might not match the nature of the change or they may actually put people off. One leader expressed to us precisely this. He said that one of the best ways to guarantee opposition to a new idea was to let certain people run with it. They would often volunteer to champion change but in doing so would alienate many others.

Effective agents are people who critique the current situation but do so with a positive spin about what could be. They might urge testing a new way of doing something or offer to investigate further an issue that they are passionate about. The key is that they are chosen by both leaders and the agents themselves and that there is no reluctance about taking it on. They can play an important role in the change:

- Shaping the aspects of the change that they are going to work on and explaining to others how it fits with the broader change.
- Encouraging others with the potential and opportunity of the change.
- Working out how best to execute and then lead that aspect of the change.
- Challenging when they feel that the implementation is falling too far short of the vision.

These people can be valuable in articulating and addressing issues in the different participant groups. However, they need to be effective with people, well-connected with others and good at gathering and using information and insight (have a high EQ). They need to bring the qualities of Maven and Connector that Malcolm Gladwell illustrates with Paul Revere in his book, *The Tipping Point*.[2]

Reference points – sounding boards

The fourth role that is sometimes present in a major change is that of a reference point. These people are those not directly involved in the change or the specific church situation but whose opinion on the context or aspects of the change is highly valued by some of the participants.

This might be a past church member who is still connected with people in the church. In a large church, it might be someone not willing to lead or not directly involved but well respected by people. It might be someone within the governance of the branch of the church involved. It can even be someone beyond the local church but in the hierarchy of the church organisation. It is someone who can exercise a degree of influence over people but who is not able or willing to follow through in any way. It is someone whom people use as a sounding board or for counsel. They might influence leaders or participants and are worth identifying and in some cases talking with, especially

146

ahead of time, to help to make the case for change and to exercise a positive influence over the change as it proceeds.

Using the roles

The primary value of understanding the roles that people play in change is in planning and in briefing and engaging with people. In big formal change programmes (e.g. for new IT systems, procedures, organisational or policy changes) these roles (or similar) are called out and people appointed to them. Although that might happen in a church setting it would be an unusual change and church. It is much more likely that people will just act out the roles. In this case, it helps the leadership team to use the role definitions to plan how to engage people in discussions. It also helps in the way that leaders interact with others. We can share our expectations of one another and give some people a better understanding of the valuable role that they are playing in the change. Planning and reflection can help to bring up questions:

- Is there a strong enough level of resolve and commitment to the end-goal amongst leaders to make this change a reality? If not, what do we alter: our resolve or the planned change?
- Is the leadership group broad enough to enable all the affected participant groups to be engaged and participate in the change effectively?
- Have we talked to all the right people and groups so that we have and can be seen to have real legitimacy in the way forward in the eyes of the participants?
- Are the best people empowered as change agents?
- Are there likely to be any reference points that we can draw on for counsel or to underpin the change?

Key point summary

- Everyone plays roles. Leaders need to identify what they are – for everyone (including themselves).
- At a summary level, people will have developed expectations based on where they feel they sit in the church community – top, middle or bottom.
- There are four important roles in a change – leaders, participants, change agents and reference points. All have responsibilities and people can play multiple roles.
- Leaders need to map out a change and plan to address each relevant group and individual.

11 - Defining the Desired Outcome

We had a new kitchen a couple of years ago. It was exciting – new units, surfaces and paint colour; a wholly different feel; lights under the wall units (we have always liked the idea of these). The change process, however, took place over two months, in the depths of one of the coldest and wettest winters we have seen for a while. We had to keep our focus on the desired outcome to weather the inconvenience cheerfully (which incidentally included cooking on the hall floor). We are not planning to do our kitchen again.

Although this book is about that painful process of change, going from something towards something else, rather than about the specific shape of the destination, there are some important features of the outcome that are worth examining. We consider these in this chapter, specifically:

- How do we know where God is leading
- Vision under development – conception
- Visions: defined collaboratively or by leaders
- The two equally important aspects of vision

Each of these topics reflects concerns that leaders have expressed when thinking through change.

How do we know where God is leading?

One of leaders' frequent concerns is (although it might be buried deeply with some): 'Are we right? Are we hearing God accurately?' Knowing that people are going to feel hurt, conflict may arise, energy and commitment to the church may drop and people may even leave, it is an important question to ask.

There is no certain way of answering the question. Indeed, even with all the details of a particular situation to hand, it can be impossible to be definitive, even for those involved. So without such certainty, sensing God's leading is a vital duty of care for anyone leading change.

Keys to providing the strongest reassurance are tied up in the origin and approach to change and include:

- A prayer-centric approach to the people, situation and environment that seeks to uncover what God is doing in the wider community and the role that the church should be playing.
- A team-based approach that involves debate and discussion to discern what is the way forward. Team reflection and discussion that tests timing, sense and direction is helpful.
- A clear fit with the specific 'why' of the church.
- Good preparation in the run-up to change that ensures an accurate view of the current reality of the church in its community and of the execution of its mission.
- Action that seeks to open up the truth and find out more – rather than conceal or smooth over. Digging for truth is a vital tool for godly dissatisfaction (see Chapter 9).
- Openness through planning and action, even to the critics. Good quality survives the heat of critical review better than poor quality. Good thinking and planning is refined not destroyed by critique.
- Humility. We are all wrong sometime and even with a careful approach we will still get it wrong and need to seek forgiveness from God and others for the ideas, words and actions that should not have been pursued.

These factors help shape the practical aspects of the change; the story of what is happening and why; the interactions and reasoning. In practice these often represent the most important aspects of being 'right'.

Follow the fruit?

An Anglican church in Derbyshire shared their dilemma with a group of other church leaders at one recent gathering.

The Sunday services were not going well or producing much fruit. They were not putting enough energy into them. On the other hand the Messy Church was flying but it was resource-heavy. Their conclusion as a group was to suggest closing Messy Church and putting resources back into the Sunday service.

Fortunately, there was a large intake of breath from the other leaders listening to this story. Their solution was to follow the fruit if resource was so tight to the Sunday service. They felt that this might be a better solution as it sacrificed what the church 'ought' to be doing for where God was bringing fruit.

Vision under development – conception

Change is closely associated with vision. Most people intuitively know what a 'vision' is: a motivating picture of what the future is going to be or should be like. Older people might recall the inspiring picture painted by Martin Luther King's 'I have a dream …' speech at the Lincoln Memorial in August 1963. Some Christians think of the Bible verse in Proverbs 29:18 (KJV), 'Where there is no vision the people perish'. In reality this 'vision' is God's revelation rather than a painting of the future. Either way, it is easy for people to see vision as a powerful and emotional picture that carries people forward.

We have always struggled with this in the context of the mostly mundane realm of organisations. This is not because we do not find pictures motivating or helpful but more because of the challenge of everyone owning the vision. In an organisational setting it is tough to co-opt people to a change in the way that comes to mind when the word vision is used, especially in our change-cynical society.

Politicians, business leaders, civic figures, analysts and pundits all paint their own compelling visions and then, far too often, leave an enormous gap between the picture and its achievement, or between the bearer of the vision and the reality of their behaviour.

In discussing change with leaders it quickly becomes clear that in most cases, outside the movies, leaders struggle to paint or 'cast' a vision that people genuinely pick up, especially in the detail that enables people to grasp it. Without the detail, it descends into slogans with little apparent depth and tends to end up being more like a specific mission rather than a vision. With too much detail, people listening become alienated by pieces of the detail and by being asked to buy into someone else's picture.

Christian leaders feel this acutely and often ask how precise and detailed the vision should be and how to get buy-in to it. The solution to this dilemma is not to go casting finished visions to the ears of unprepared people.

If 'vision' is the finished painting then 'conception' is the sketching of the ideas and line drawings that go before it. Whilst leaders might need to paint the final picture on their own (at least in a large group) everyone can input to the drawings. This works well when the church is committed to its 'why'. It helps people 'bite' when the final vision is cast.

Visions rarely come fully formed to some select group anyway. Just like strategies in most businesses, they evolve from a process of learning, reflection and assessment.[1] In church they arise best from insights that people contribute when they add their perspective and subject it to God's leading.

We should therefore find ways to capture this dynamic by outlining ideas and thinking and inviting input from the church. Through this process the elements of the vision can be developed and refined, and people see parts that they feel they have contributed or shaped. Details can be changed and adjusted as the change being conceived evolves in the light of discussion, inputs and tests.

Then, when the vision is finally (in as much as it is ever final) painted it can be richer and fuller, more detailed and more readily owned. People will also be much clearer about the fact that a vision is a painting of the future, it is not the future in its precise detail.

It is important to have this period of conception and the evolving clarity of God's leading before producing a vision. This is the same as artists when they write a novel, paint a picture or sculpt stone.

Visions: defined collaboratively or by leaders?

It is perhaps worth spending a little longer on a question that comes up repeatedly in sessions with leaders. Does a leader or the leaders provide the vision or should we involve the church?

Despite what we have said so far, there is no definitive right answer to this question for every church situation. One leader concerned at the discussion about collaboration wanted to know whether their own approach in their church had been right. She shared that the people had pressed her to make the decisions, without their input. They simply wanted direction. They had welcomed her decisions and direction. It was evident in her explanation of what had happened that the church had clearly moved forward and grown numerically and in confidence. For the time and place it was evident that her approach had been effective, welcomed by the church and that they had adopted the vision wholeheartedly.

This example emphasises that in change there are only guides and few if any hard and fast rules. However, there are reasons why generally it is important that we involve people as early as possible in shaping change:

We are one interdependent fellowship

Jesus emphasised the power and importance of unity.[2] Paul speaks of the interdependence of the church as the body of Christ.[3] We are encouraged to become mature and effective disciples.[4] This allows every place for leadership and godly influence but at the same time it is a picture of interdependence and growth. It does not fit with leaders disempowering the body with a 'tell-sell' model of visioning and change.

No involvement means no engagement

In our society, with its strong emphasis on the individual, on education and on freedom, people make choices over almost all aspects of their lives. In such a situation, the role and challenge of leading is to encourage positive choices from people so that they wholeheartedly participate, not merely turn up. This helps to ensure that everyone lives out being church when together and on their own. We become what we decide, not what we are told. As Stephen Covey has said, 'Without involvement, there is no commitment. Mark it down, asterisk it, circle it, underline it. No involvement, no commitment.'

Missed opportunity

It is scary to involve people because there will be differences of view, conflict and objections. However, this is inevitable in change. It will happen sooner or later wherever people need to transition and commit. Early involvement helps people to transition and, done wisely, can also help build unity amongst divergent views.

The weakness of 'vision casting'

One approach to vision development and realisation is to use a closed process limited to a few people. The vision is then worked up and 'cast' at the now fashionable annual event of 'Vision Sunday'. This brings with it significant weaknesses.

At one church we know, the vision had been worked up between minister and PCC. There had been some consultation but the actual development of the vision was done by a few to introduce at Vision Sunday.

Although the vision had been given much thought and a lot of work had gone into both its shape and the presentation of it, the result was still that the 'caster' of the vision saw it as of much greater importance than the majority of the congregation. The response to the vision, which was expected to be engagement and enthusiasm, was not forthcoming.

The services did not catch those away that weekend, there was no discussion or engagement on the importance of the vision and the response remained muted. The result has been slow progress to the realisation of the vision and a persistent difficulty in connecting the vision and the church programme.

Involvement does not mean a free-for-all. It does not mean that everyone gets what they want (otherwise change would be almost impossible). It does not mandate the way the final decision is arrived at and it needs a good structure in a large group.

It requires orchestration and honest, open engagement by the leaders and it means that the way that change is led typically needs to integrate seamlessly into a well-functioning leadership structure, so that the communication and organisation tasks happen early enough to enable involvement.

Even leaders in commercial organisations recognise this reality. As the rate of technological and market change has continued to accelerate and businesses need to be much more adaptable, their structure has become flatter and decisions need to be made closer to the point where a business touches its markets. Senior leaders do not have the information, time or skills to make the right decisions themselves.

This need is expressed in many approaches: adaptive leadership; conversational leadership; systems approaches to change and learning; and development programmes that focus on interpersonal skills. At their root these share a common thread in helping people engage effectively with each other and, despite different roles and status, make open and informed decisions.

Even in larger churches, there are many ways that involvement can be secured:

- Open meetings that gather views, present information and help people to build a common picture. Even large numbers can be managed in 'post-it' note gathering sessions which can both engage and energise.
- Consultation papers (like British government 'green papers').
- Questionnaires or small group sessions which secure individual or group responses to questions defined by the leadership team.
- Consultation with different groups in the church, where a leader goes to one of their meetings to talk with them and find out their thoughts (home groups, choir, service leaders, musicians, youth workers, children's workers, etc.).

These activities are a lot of work, which is why they are sometimes ignored. An open decision process brings work and many benefits. It tests the ideas and shape of change. It builds up the case for change. It increases the level of leadership certainty

156

and urgency. Open consultation does not mean that leaders cannot develop views about the way forward and argue their case but it is important that others in the church are given the space and information to think through the issue and that as the leaders argue their case they advocate it, inviting open challenge and query. It is when leaders try to close down conversations that commitment is lost. Commitment is after all a choice.

The two equally important aspects of vision

Very often visions focus on 'hard' factors, perhaps because of the left-brained orientation of many church leaders or the felt need to make the outcome as tangible and real as possible. By 'hard' we mean tangible items: services, buildings, numbers, specific activities or groups – items that can be seen and counted. They much less prominently or frequently focus on the 'soft' factors: qualities, way of being, values, climate and culture. This is a mistake. Most of the envisioning in the Bible is about these softer facets of life. In our experience it is easier for people to engage with and addresses these often more important topics.

When thinking about the desired outcome, leaders need to explicitly consider both hard and soft elements and make sure that the important items – not only the ones that can be enumerated – stay the important items.

As that artist of artists, Albert Einstein, wisely said, 'Everything that can be counted does not necessarily count; everything that counts cannot necessarily be counted.' Soft factors often need more work to be painted well but the reward is worth every bit of the effort.

A rounded development of vision, such as would come from the vision drivers (bold in the diagram), will inevitably include both hard and soft elements. With this in mind there are therefore two aspects to the vision that are worth considering.

157

1. The nature of the change – the target state

It is not possible to be prescriptive. Change can encompass anything, and the vision is a work of creation and discernment so each should be unique. In fact, its uniqueness and sharp edges mark it out as having real value. If a vision is so general that everyone will agree with it, then it is no use as a destination or in defining the steps to the future. The questions that trigger such a picture are, for example:

- How do we (collectively) want the place to be?
- What will be its purpose?
- What will it look like?
- What activity will be going on and not going on?
- How will it be organised or structured?
- What are the key building blocks?

These need to be worked through all the way to their implications.

It easy to underestimate the amount of thought and discussion that is needed to get a clear picture and what it really means. However, the clearer the end state, the easier it is to manage the change effectively because it unlocks insight, for the stakeholders, in the change and their potential interests and perspectives during the conception stage. It also makes the change more real and bounded, important characteristics for success.

It is important that the vision is realistic. Some visions are not. They are obviously impractical, poorly thought through or shaped by unfortunate circumstance. By realism we mean that it makes sense and is realistic in faith. It is bold and expresses the hope and leading of God, not the papering over of poor strategic thinking.

2. The way of being – culture

The way of being is the alter ego of the target state. It comprises most of the soft factors that people often steer away from. Yet, as mentioned, these are vitally important. God made us as human beings and our call is most particularly about a call to be with him.

In the same vein these soft factors are often the most powerful elements of any change. Many changes in companies, government bodies and churches do not seem to have touched some of the deep cultural facets of the organisation. Much of what is sold as change by leaders seems superficial. Even in 1980, people in Britain complained about the NHS and its inefficiency and bureaucracy. There have been myriad changes since but over thirty years on, and with reviews like that conducted into Mid-Staffs in 2013, we can see how resistant the behaviour and culture of a human organisation can be.

Our experience is that the underlying values and approach are highly resistant to change. Values reappear under stress. Yet this 'way of being' is the most important aspect of an organisation. For churches, becoming more welcoming, more united or more prayerful might be key aspects of any change. These things therefore need to be in the vision. The soft side of the vision can be provoked by questions such as:

- How will we behave as church?
- What will be the characteristics of our meetings?
- What are the goals for us as disciples and as a community?
- How will it feel?
- How will newcomers experience this?
- How will conflict be resolved? (Is it different from the past?)
- Are there lifestyle goals that we are aiming for as a community or as individuals?

The debate and definition of this will flesh out the human skills, outlook and climate that is desired (typically through and beyond change) which is often poorly defined by leaders, who may fixate on the tangible, structural or organisational changes that are needed.

One final point on vision. One change expert, Daryl Conner,[5] suggests that leaders need to be particularly concerned about 'future shock' – when people can no longer assimilate change without being dysfunctional because its demands exceed their capacity to cope.

This highlights an important point. Vision should be a stretch. It should rest on faith. But it still needs to be carefully and prayerfully crafted and described so that it does not leave people behind. When it comes to actions and timescales there needs to be a careful definition of what should be achieved and by when so that people do not check out early on in the process.

Key point summary

- Leaders who want to make sure a change is 'right' should look to the process they follow and the fit with the church 'why'.
- Visions are never finished. They should be preceded by conception and continue to be shaped even after they are shared.
- Ideally, visions should be generated collaboratively, expressed creatively and spoken of repeatedly.
- Visions should include both a target state and a way of being, expressing the hard and soft aspects of the goal.

12 - Design for Success

It is too easy, when you feel responsible for something, for it to sit centre stage in your mind. As a result you can be holding in your head a clear picture of what it happening and when. Yet for most people in church, almost every change will be another thing going on in their lives and they will be paying a certain amount of attention to it but are unlikely to keep it at the top of their minds. Inevitably this makes bigger changes confusing and muddled, and participants get frustrated by this.

It is important that frustration is not allowed to build up unnecessarily. This means that the supporting structures for change need to be well designed and work effectively. In particular, that:

- Communications are imaginative and clear.
- Communications reflect how people adopt change.
- Governance is well understood.
- The change is launched well.
- Activity is well organised.

This will maximise the probability of the change achieving its goals and help people to buy in and stay on board.

Communications are imaginative and clear

Conversational communications
Good communication is one of the most important factors for making change work smoothly. Leaders recognise its importance. It prevents unnecessary disconnects and friction. Indeed, it is amongst the most frequently cited lessons from change that Arrow leaders highlighted.

People need continual encouragement and reinforcement of the direction of the church and where the change sits within this. They need to be reminded of the goal, know that the leadership see the change as important, understand why it is important and be reminded of the value it adds. It is remarkably easy for congregations to lose sight of all this, especially where people attend less than weekly, or where the change is in a part of the church's work that is only visible to a subsection (e.g. its youth and children's work, aspects of its outreach or social work).

Sowing seed for future changes

At one Anglican church, the minister was keen to explore allowing children to take Communion and participate fully in the service even when quite young. He recognised that this would be something that the leaders would need to support fully if it was to be introduced successfully and not generate resistance from different groups in church.

So he explored the subject with the PCC, with questions like, 'Can you tell me the theological justification for not giving Communion, if we do infant baptism?' He made no proposal to change and simply asked leaders to reflect on the discussion in the meeting and afterwards, giving them the opportunity to hear his thinking on the 'why' and to discuss their thoughts. His aim was, 'to explore it, in a spirit of unity' and give everyone chance to discuss the topic.

There was a lot of disagreement but it was expressed constructively because of the context. Two meetings further on, another member of the staff team gave his theological reflections on the subject. The discussion continued outside meetings between individuals for over a year.

Then it was raised by someone else at a later meeting and the PCC unanimously chose to introduce it. It was a similarly smooth process of introduction as the church brought it into its worship.

The unpressured space given to leaders to consider the change gave them opportunity to think through their own position and encouraged discussion which honed their thinking. The result was that a potentially controversial change was enthusiastically and unitedly adopted by the church.

This is a role that is wisely allocated to someone specifically on the leadership group – not necessarily to communicate directly but to make sure that it is being done well and at the right frequency.

The most effective communications are frequent (almost to overkill), a mixture of the general and the targeted, and often face-to-face. These chime with best practices for innovation in companies that emphasise the value of frequent, informal and face-to-face communications for bringing new products, services and systems to market.

However, we are frequently asked, 'What is the best way to execute this in a church setting?' The default approach is not the best.

One-way, broadcast methods – sermons, notices, general newsletters or web pages that are updated – address the whole of the church with facts, events, rationale and decisions. It is a good start but in no way reflects what Arrow leaders picked out as effective in their review of well-managed changes. They highlighted effective communications as:

- Individual or small meetings to discuss delicate or difficult aspects of the changes. These permit a genuinely interactive exchange that gives people the feeling that their views are heard. This is often done where individuals are particularly sensitive or greatly impacted. For instance, in one case, during a change in leadership structure one of the leaders visited every key member of a small church to both make sure that they heard the facts of the change and to listen and demonstrate his listening to their concerns and responses.
- Discussions directly with the different groups involved so that, 'what it really means for us' is understood and, where necessary, a course correction is made (e.g. talking

with the choir, or the home group leaders on the practical details).

- Specially organised meetings where the change is examined, prayed about and talked through, with feedback being aired amongst the whole group and specific action points captured.
- A clear structure of responsibilities so that people know who is supposed to be doing what for the change (see governance later). Sometimes this is separate from the day-to-day leadership team as in the case of several churches that used this approach for changes in location or buildings or another that used it for a change in the Sunday worship services. These groups then communicate both generally through the normal means but also used special slots, consultation sessions and small group dialogues.

Although much of this appears informal, in almost all cases we have experienced, whoever felt responsible for the change was actually doing the communications in a structured manner – to make sure that they did not forget anyone and to ensure that the frequency and completeness of the communications was tight.

This becomes especially important when a change is contentious. Here, opportunity is needed to engage especially with those groups who are unhappy. This maximises the likelihood that the relationship will be maintained and that an agreement can be reached on the way forward. It needs good planning and a determination to try to engage even those people who don't like the change and want to fight it (see Chapter 5 on the leaders approach to those who disagree).

Clearly, where special meetings or an open invitation is offered to people they may choose not to attend. In these cases the only approach is a direct one to those who are unhappy but

165

seem unwilling to try to get resolution in the forums offered. Leaders need to try this although it does not mean that it will work.

All this reflects a strongly conversational approach to communications rather than a broadcast programme. The wider, general communications are important to maintain visibility and help keep people on roughly the same page with progress but they can never substitute for dialogue. Good communications is a big time commitment. There is no shortcut to this. It is why the leadership only has so much capacity to launch and lead change, otherwise it becomes swamped, especially if the change is a controversial one.

Expressing the desired outcome
'The soul never thinks without a picture.'
Aristotle

There are more ways to express vision than can be summarised in a book. Despite this it always surprises us that most visions seem to be simple written statements, most often no more than a side of paper, sometimes more bullet points than a picture. We seem to have given up our creative side in the way that most churches present them – hardly multimedia, little poetry, few pictures (ironically), no story.

We have seen many different and creative ways used to express a vision – and creativity is worth applying if the vision is to be an important aspect of church life for a few years and if the typically varied congregation is to relate to it well. More varieties of expression are better than fewer. Here are just a few examples, firstly from the corporate world:

- The use of a story format or narrative that either looks forwards or backwards to explain the significance of the change and its development and impact. We have seen this done in a newsletter format, with interviews, comments, photos, etc. It provides a neat reference point for people if produced early enough in a change and it underpins the rationale for what is going on.

- A comic/cartoon style of brochure that explains the same issues as above. One client, a beer producer, created a pamphlet called 'Our brew' that was distributed to all relevant employees and explained the most important aspects of the behavioural change and how it related to the business and its success.
- Pictures or paintings. One client produced a wall display with the change pictured as a river and waterfall that the organisation was going through (in a barrel!) showing different aspects of the change, the challenges (rocks in the river) and what was being done to address them (ropes, poles and boats).
- A 'day-in-the-life-of ...' (DILO) cameo. We have seen this done in written form, as screenshots on a computer screen or as a storyboard that describe how the change will impact a particular role or event in the life of the organisation. These cameos illustrate scenarios that show behaviour. We have even seen one of these turned into an immersive experience with actors and props, and others put into videos (typically when they need to be distributed over distances). This highlights the important changes, shows what it will be like when it is all stabilised and illustrates the potential benefits.
- Asking people to draw pictures of how things currently are and how they need to change. We have seen these describing the planning or product development processes in business, or how sales works. They are often cartoon-style illustrations that can use humour to put into pictures what many people are thinking.
- Photo montages – or as agencies call them 'mood boards'.

167

In each case these approaches allow for a before and after picture and can be used as formats for updating people as things progress through the change. The variety of approaches not only helps to keep people engaged and interested (above and beyond a simple verbal or written update, which people often seem to miss) but also helps people with different communication styles to hook into the change and understand its implications and value all the way through its implementation. In a church context examples of imaginative communications might include:

- The use of drama or sketches in services and meetings, sometimes including DILO or 'week in the life' type scenarios for home groups, children's and youth activities, services and the like.
- Modelling aspects of the vision with one-off events that illustrate how it might be, e.g. a new service.
- Use of analogies or stories (the Bible has a few ...).
- Borrowing benchmarks, e.g. our welcome desk should be like the Apple store.
- Names and pictures, e.g. 'café' church ... coffee shop.
- Short 'talking heads' or docu-interview style videos that comment on events, progress and people's experience.
- External presentations, e.g. from architects if the project is about buildings, other churches or specialists.
- An away-day type of event (like in the Alpha course) – with a more immersive style of communication and interaction.
- Special event evenings that illustrate the future experience (different from a pilot in that they have been specifically badged as a chance to experience it).

Parallels can also be used effectively. For example, if we were Pret A Manger what would our welcome look like? How would it be organised? How is what we are doing similar? We want the service to have the same sense of special event as Spring Harvest, so we are doing it like this?

Using these sorts of communication approaches helps to both engage and inform and the variety works to help different groups in the church to latch on to what is happening and its significance. Using only one method repeatedly quickly exhausts people's interest.

Communications reflect how people adopt change

We are probably all intuitively familiar with the diffusion curve. This represents how a group of people will respond to any innovation. It is typically seen as a standard bell curve.

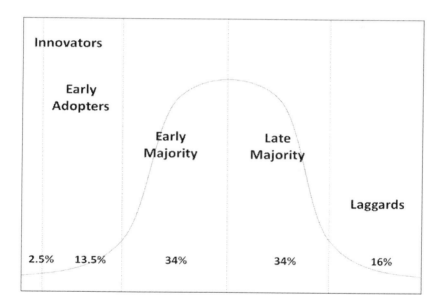

There will be the innovators who eagerly adopt the change. These will be followed quickly by the early adopters. Together these are the archetypal ~15% who will respond the most positively to new things. The next ~70% will split into the early and late majority who will follow on at differing speeds to take on something new. The final ~15% are called the laggards.

169

In today's society, they might still not have a DVD player, may not want or use a mobile phone or refuse to recycle.

This curve is a useful representation of how people will typically group in their response to changes in church. The dispersion of responses is in the nature of a population. Leaders can expect that only in rare exceptions will this not be the case. Its real value is in showing what to expect from people and how to handle their responses depending upon where they sit on the curve.

Important points are:

- People do not always fall into the same segment of the curve for every change (despite what you may think). Whilst people are naturally more conservative or innovative, their response to a specific change isn't always the same. It is important that leaders do not pre-judge where people will sit but rather find out.
- The curve demonstrates that in a successful change most people will change their minds. Their response alters with time, information and experience. Persistence and making the change work helps people to accept and adopt it but they do so at different speeds.
- Different people look for different evidence before they commit. In particular those later down the curve will not commit until others have done so and have proved the value of change. Communication of different elements in the change through time can help this process.
- Some people, the laggards, are highly likely never to adopt the change. There will almost always be some who do not transition.
- At the start, although leaders should speak to everyone, the key conversations are with those at the front of the curve. The others will not really hear the arguments. These innovators and early adopters respond to different

messages and this means that the messages need to change over time to match the fact that people listen for different things depending on where they are in the adoption cycle.

The sort of things that the different segments of the curve are interested in are:

- Innovators: these people may well be the enthusiasts for the topic, issue or technology that is involved in the change (e.g. audio-visual methods, song styles, music format, video, green issues, coffee. (We jest not ... have you met any Australians recently?). The latest ideas in this area will often appeal. The idea of being first with something, and novelty, has a positive appeal.
- Early Adopters: unlike the innovators, to whom the idea appeals because of its novelty and intrinsic appeal, this segment is more likely to see the change as the gateway to change in further aspects of church. Perhaps a bit more visionary in their outlook, they like the uniqueness of what is being done and the influence that being early to approve gives them.
- Early Majority: this group will often contain key church leaders. They like to see change as an evolution not revolution and therefore that an appropriate pace is set. As a result they want changes to be practical and useful. They like to adopt things that seem proven and safe so they like pilots or benchmarks from other churches or environments that reduce the risk of change. They like niggles to be sorted out before they buy in.
- Late Majority: this is another large segment of the church population but it differs from the early majority in being more conservative. They are less keen on the disruption and the losses that change generates and may see issues with loyalty to people or activities that are being changed. They value continuity and are more concerned about cost.

They can be critical of teething troubles, seeing them as an unacceptable price of change.

- Laggards: this segment are the arch sceptics of the change or those with an innate dislike of it. They may retain serious and important criticisms of it. They may be timid or aggressive about what is being lost. Their viewpoint is an extreme that may never shift throughout the change which can be discouraging.

It can be helpful for leaders to try to place vocal critics of a change on the curve to judge whether their views are likely to alter. Not everyone will accept change. A few will always mourn their losses and dislike the change. This is a logical consequence of free choice. They do not have to support it. Some will prefer to have nothing to do with it or only accept grudgingly.

The curve does helpfully show the pattern by which change builds in a community. Just as we see in society at large with fashion or colour trends and with the spread of new technologies, we will see the same with people's attitudes to change in church and their acceptance of new things.

Governance is well understood

Often in church, a special governance structure is used only for exceptional projects, notably reordering or rebuilding. So, for instance, at the moment in one of our churches we are working on a rebuilding project and this has a separate small team that is handling all aspects of the proposed change – liaising with the contractors and handling fundraising, building design, queries, questions and planning.

This is a great structure to consider for these sorts of changes because it provides a lot of clarity for the church about who to talk with, responsibilities and actions. As a result of this it tends to provoke more questions and deliver greater transparency. This is good. Even a question is a certain amount of commitment and interest and can be relatively easy to generate.

However, churches rarely seem to use these sort of 'pop-up' structures for other sorts of change. We know of some that have used the same approach for changes to the service pattern and others that have used it for mission but it tends to be used in a limited way. More often the change will be left within the ordinary governance structure, if not with the main governing body then with a sub-committee or working party.

This can miss an opportunity to flag the significance of the change and also means that the leaders for the change are normally those who are incumbent in the overall group – sometimes not the best people to take on the specifics of the change. Ideally leaders want enthusiastic, persuasive change agents engaged in the leading of the change.

It is worth considering this approach for a much wider range of changes than most churches do at the moment.

The change is launched well

Biting the bullet quickly

Starting well, positioning the change realistically, and choosing what actions are taken when, can all help to ensure that the commitment to change is easier to build.

The sequence of events in an extended process of change is important. In human terms a real change will generate pain and it is difficult to put up with this pain when you feel that there is a choice. So choosing to bite the bullet early on some of the most painful items can be important to sustaining the change. If they are not dealt with early then they may never be dealt with. If they are sorted early, people are more likely to forget the pain and find it easier to focus on the upsides in the change. This is why effective leaders often tackle the most difficult topics early.

For instance, in one church where the need to move forward involved a transformation of the music and reordering of the chancel, one of the earliest actions of the leadership was to abolish the choir and press for a redesign of this area in the building. These were tackled early to take what was a painful decision for some when there was the energy to do this. Had it been mooted later then there would have been many, already weary from earlier battles, who would not have been prepared to take on a challenge of this size.

So initiating change might involve identifying the key symbols or artefacts of the past that need to go and removing these early. These can be physical items (pews, decoration, literature), procedures (meetings, practices, rotas) or behaviours (terminology, liturgy). The key items are those that compromise the expectations or standards that are embodied in the change or the purpose of the church.

Some of these can be small but still important. For example, in one church seeking to enhance the quality of their welcome and hospitality, changing the quality of the coffee and abolishing the practice of putting out a bowl to collect donations were important changes for the messages that they sent to visitors and newcomers who decided to stay for refreshments. They also set the tone for the church.

These need to be identified and then leaders must be consistent in securing them and ensuring no back-tracking. This is not as easy as it sounds. It can require the vigilance and persistence of a strong school teacher to make sure that expectations are really upheld. The challenge is not always because people object to the changes. Rather it can be that people, not knowing what is now being done, do what they remember from before.

Continuity vs breaking with the past

Care is needed over the positioning of changes. There may be things that need to stop in the life of the church but this should not always be projected as a break with the past. This can be unhelpful. A rejection of important and often previously valuable practices risks hurting people unnecessarily. It can also fail to latch onto the motivations that people bring for supporting the change, which are most likely to be in a new application of a value that they already hold.

Where honest, it is useful to demonstrate the continuity and linkage with the past, even as the new is brought in and replaces it. Leaders should seek opportunities to identify the value that people saw in what has gone before wherever possible. This acknowledges both people and values important to the church and the future. It may even demonstrate some of the values that the future is supposed to represent.

Indeed, this can be very helpful. In one church where the decision to move from uniformed organisations to other new children's and youth groups, the passing of what was recognised as great work was marked in a special set of Sunday celebrations and recognition of those who had given so much to the work.

Announcing

Leaders need to decide whether to announce an overarching change and if so when. Just because leaders are wanting to move forward it does not necessarily mean that it is important to call these things out as a change. Some of the most profound changes do not get announced or decided upon until after they have happened and we recognise the wider significance of them. This can be particularly true where the change is less an envisioned move forward and more the selection of some clear initial steps that the church wants to take under God.

Sometimes an announcement gets in the way. It allows things to be put it in a box and challenged. It can mobilise opponents and distract leaders from focusing on the key actions of the moment. It can prevent the adoption of powerful changes that bubble up in a community and which can create real steps forward in the life of the church. It may be the adoption of an all-church, mid-week prayer or teaching meeting, someone's enthusiasm for creating a prayer room, promoting prayer triplets, reinvigorating intercessions in the Sunday service or whatever God is leading parts of the congregation to do.

Naming a change as such should only be done if it is useful. The decision then needs to be taken when to publicly introduce a change and how to articulate the rationale for it. In our experience this is sometimes done too early. It is as if we feel that we need to do something and, rather than sticking with the first step, we say something bold. This can often constrain change.

Launch tactics

There are many ways to launch a change. Typically they are best launched by helping the church to focus on the critical issues or concerns that are driving the change. This requires people's attention to be drawn to the area of the church's life and work that the leaders feel God is wanting to move forward. Good starting points include surveys and research by groups from the congregation, targeted at specific topics. Similarly, reviews conducted as a part of any regular planning cycle in the church or set up as a subgroup of the church council can play a similar role.

For reviews to be effective it is important that a wide enough remit is given to the group and that there is leadership team representation on the group. If the process is conducted in an open fashion, it can stimulate and inform the church as it goes forward.

Other ways to start change can be through using key meetings to raise questions and provoke thought on key aspects of church life. This allows time and space for people to consider a topic they have never thought about or recognised and to reflect on the importance and potential implications of the questions raised. It may need to be done repeatedly if it is to start the church really thinking. Few people immediately absorb new topics and questions will need to provoke if people are really to start to move.

The power of the experiment

Often people will give you permission to change if it is an experiment that will be assessed over a given period of time.

At one church that felt the need to make a change that would affect the children's ministry, one longstanding member of the church said that, if it went ahead, he and his family would consider leaving the church.

One of the leaders said that the church was going to experiment with a new model and would value his assessment at the end. He was more than happy with this. It kept him in the loop and he looked forward to being proved right. However, at the end of the time, the assessment was hardly needed. He spontaneously indicated how happy his own children were with the new model.

The experiment gave him the time, learning and freedom to come to terms with the change.

With some topics it is possible for leaders to try things and see how they work. This might involve piloting a new service format to see how it goes, providing samples of new study materials, tagging a new event on to a well-established one, giving someone a specific new role for a season only. Some things can be tried to allow the church to reflect on it, refine it or drop it if it does not work well.

Often great ideas for change can bubble up within a group and if leaders are timely and sensitive, people can be encouraged to try their idea out. The advantage of this approach is that there is little at stake for either leaders or members. Yet, if worthwhile, this small step opens up formal adoption by the church.

Activity is well organised

Change needs to be well organised yet as John Kotter[1] has commented, 'Examining close to one hundred cases (of major change), I found that most people did not handle large scale change well ... they made predictable mistakes.' Many of these are relatively simple aspects of organisation.

Planning and organisation

Many of the lessons about change revolve around good organisation and a positive and respectful approach towards people. For change, good organisation means the basic skills of managing a project need to be approached professionally:

- Defining what the change is about.
- Identifying the 'milestone' markers that need to be reached as it progresses.
- Putting together a realistic plan with all the right people.
- Allocating roles, responsibilities and timings.
- Establishing a regular means of review and management.
- Communicating effectively.

These basics fix a lot of what goes wrong unnecessarily and reflect lessons from many of the management surveys conducted into change (see Chapter 13). These basics provide a foundation for the effective use of the approach to change outlined in this book. No amount of careful handling of people and planning on the soft aspects of the change will compensate if the practical tasks are handled badly. Much of this can be avoided if leaders plan properly.

Practical steps

Leaders should seek to involve in the planning people who can grapple well with these disciplines if they themselves struggle. However, it is vital that these people do not only bring a toolbox of techniques. This can easily result in an over-sophisticated or jargon-ridden paper plan that has little value or connection to the change. It is vital that if someone with these skills joins the team they are as motivated and committed to the outcome as others and that they work hand-in-glove with the rest of the team to produce a simple plan that reflects the combined views of the best way forward. The result should be that the output could be 'understood by my mum' (as one consultant we know always used to say).

Another way that we have found to help unlock this area of planning is to do a mental walk through and, on your own or with others, visualise the change one step at a time. As this is talked through, it should highlight dependencies when things need to happen. It will also highlight areas of risk, ways that things could go wrong or be missed and can help with developing a checklist of items to review regularly to make sure that risks are managed.

The value of planning

One church engaged in the Lead Academy process was looking at major changes in its future. These landmarks included the creation of a proper leadership team, radical change in its house groups and additions to the staff team.

Its review of the risks and of past changes in the church quickly identified potential problems in securing the right finance for the change and in making sure that the leaders in the church really signed up for the realities of what would be involved in the decision-making and ministry changes.

Previous changes had, with hindsight, gone astray because no timescales had been put on the key changes and leaders had not held themselves accountable for achieving the plans that had been discussed.

This led the leaders to decide that a much clearer and more transparent planning process was a critical part of helping to make the vision a reality for the church.

Risk registers

Finally, it is worth considering the use of a risk register. In running projects, one of the things that helps to ensure that important items do not get missed is when leaders sit down and think about where things are most likely to go wrong. This can be done by reviewing the visualisation mentioned above or by thinking about each aspect of the change – people (groups, individuals, etc.), places, communications, skills, events, equipment, materials, etc. – or simply to discuss it with your 'black hats' on.[2]

For each item it should be possible to work out a way to reduce the risk. It is unlikely that you can eliminate every risk but there is almost always something that can be done to minimise it. Then write each risk down with the way that it might be minimised and review this on a regular basis throughout the change. This risk register is one of the basics of project management that, if well-constructed, is very useful.

Key point summary

- Use both broadcast and conversational communications. Imaginative, two-way methods are the most effective.
- People naturally adopt change at different speeds and for different reasons. Leaders need to anticipate this in the way that they communicate.
- Governance for change is important in building and maintaining commitment. It helps if it is clear to all the church
- Change can be started with an announcement, an experiment or just a few specific steps.
- Change needs effective organisation – scoping, clear steps and roles – and regular review.

13 - Embrace Risk

It is a fact of life. People are risk-averse. Social scientists have long recognised this and built it into their models of human behaviour. We prefer to have a sure result rather than an uncertain one. We prefer not to lose something rather than to gain the equivalent amount. A simple illustration: given the choice, would you prefer a gift of £50, or to play a game with a 50% chance of winning £120? In classical economics and logic it would seem best to choose the second option, since the average pay-off of £60 is bigger for the average person (especially if you are allowed to play 4 or 5 times). However, in practice, most people choose the first option. They would prefer to have a smaller but absolutely sure payment rather than a bigger but more uncertain one. In our minds, that makes sense – it is a bird in the hand.

So when considering change, where new and uncertain avenues are being pursued, it is not surprising that leaders (and congregations) become much more sensitive to risk and uncertainty. Sadly, this is not the best strategy. Too often the greatest risk that any organisation faces is the risk of ineffectiveness.

In this chapter, we want to encourage leaders, including ourselves, to embrace risk rather than seek to avoid it. This is surprisingly the logical response. We are not suggesting a cavalier approach, merely a positive and engaging one. We will explain our reasons for this and the best way to handle risks under five headings:

- Our walk is not about success and failure.
- Change fails – so change more frequently.

- Beware the most common change risks.
- Learn from your church's history.
- Use risks as signposts to shape change management.

Our walk is not about success and failure

> 'God does not require that we be successful
> only that we be faithful.'
>
> *Mother Theresa*

We should be wary of thoughts of success and failure. We can be easily discouraged from trying something that we feel might fail, especially if we have a perfectionist or people-pleasing streak. Society inflates the importance of success such that it can be difficult to retain a true bearing on what we should be doing. Sometimes we cannot see the value that God can in things that 'fail'.

He doesn't call us to succeed but to be faithful and there are many examples of ministry in the Bible that would be judged as anything but successful, especially when considering Israel's prophets in the Old Testament. Yet these were faithful servants of God and we are likewise called to follow God's lead, regardless of the probability of success and despite the risks.

God wants his church to be his body working for the change that he wants in the world. However, God plays a long game and so we should recognise that embarking on change may not produce the outcomes that we expect, when we expect them. The imperative comes from God and our need to engage with a changing society and environment. We will be failing if we do not lead congregations into change.

Change fails – so change more frequently

'Success consists of going from failure to
failure without loss of enthusiasm.'

Winston Churchill

'The way to succeed is to double your
failure rate.'

Thomas Watson (Founder of IBM)

All change-management approaches make a lot of risk management. Risk analysis, risk registers and the relatively recently defined discipline of risk management all testify to this. Health-and-safety ways of working have shaped our environment and approach – all with the purpose that we minimise risks to life, limb and litigation. Overall this is a good thing, although taken to extremes it can be unhealthy. Often it can seem that we review risks only to avoid taking action. That is not useful.

The hard fact is that in human terms there is a better than even chance that any change we lead will fail. So as a leader over your lifetime you can expect to fail quite often. The salutary truth is that the only way not to fail is not to try.

Failure should not be the concern. As William G. T. Shedd once wrote, 'Ships are safest in harbour but ships were not built to stay in harbour ...' So as leaders we need to become used to failing. Do not be fooled by the stories written by leaders who seem to have failed with their initiatives infrequently, if at all. This must surely be where reality and presentation diverge. A wide range of studies suggests otherwise:

- Change programmes fail on two out of three occasions (e.g. Kotter, Balogun and Hope Hailey, 2004).
- Mergers and acquisitions do not create the value expected 70% of the time (e.g. McKinsey, 2010).
- Large IT implementations have low success rates. Sometimes we read about the bigger failures in

newspapers, as with recent BBC or NHS programmes. In 2002 *Fortune* magazine quoted research by the Standish Group that found that of 280,000 IT projects, only 78,000 were classified as successful (~25%). Other studies of ERP systems implementations (the large systems that enable businesses to manage their day-to-day transactions and accounts) are routinely below 40%. Customer management systems are the same. In 2002 Gartner, another analyst group, found that 55% of all installations of customer-relationship software, probably the hottest turn-of-the-millennium corporate IT fad, did not produce any results.

- A 2008 study of 1500 practitioners of change in businesses around the globe by the Institute of Business Value at IBM found that 59% of projects failed (but the variation in company success rates was between 80% and 8%, suggesting more elements of controllability than many might think).
- The Economist Intelligence Unit conducted an international survey on business change initiatives in 2010 (288 managers) where executives reckoned that no more than 40% of change initiatives in the last 5 years had been successful.
- In 2012, the McKinsey-Oxford study reviewed 5,400 IT projects and found that 45% had a cost overrun and 56% underachieved the target benefits.
- Studies on innovation and business start-ups also suggest high rates of failure.

Some Christian leaders have been upset by these facts when we talk about change – as if it is not helpful to point out the risks and it only serves to discourage. However, this is not really the point of the statistics. They provide some important take-aways:

- If we want success then we need to introduce more changes not fewer. In this way we will have more successful ones. Persistence is important. As Thomas Edison once said, 'I failed my way to success.' A key lesson is to lead more change. This way we will uncover better ways of taking forward the mission of the church. Less change is less opportunity to discover the ways that work.
- Failure is best treated in the same way as resistance (Chapter 4). It is feedback to learn from. This is the lesson that some of the most innovative businesses emphasise.[1]

So be prepared to fail and do not be worried about this. Failure will sometimes partner faithfulness. We should be effective stewards, as focused and committed as entrepreneurs in pressing forward despite the odds. Staying still has risks. The risks here are substantial if perhaps a little less visible or fast-acting. The best way to avoid failing is not to try anything new but of course this is really to fail most profoundly.

Valuing the lessons of failure

Recently we were privileged to hear from an ex-director of Microsoft. He described Microsoft as an organisation that honoured failure. The root of this attitude is that failure is the key to learning.

If you fail but learn from your failure you are applauded but if you succeed and learn nothing you are likely to be in trouble. Why do they have this attitude? Because Bill Gates has a scientific background and all scientific progress is made on the foundation of failure. You learn by failing until you succeed.

Interestingly, he went on to make the following observation: 'It seems to me looking in from outside that the church is afraid of failure. Someone has an idea but it fails. There is heavy criticism and nobody dares try again. No wonder you do not make much progress.'

Beware the most common change risks

Risk assessment should be done once the goal of change is clear. This will help to identify the specific real concerns that need to be mitigated (see previous chapter). However, there are some risks that seem to be common, highlighted by various studies of change and imprinted by our own experience. Our personal top five are:

1. *The lack of coherent leadership resolve.* An enormous amount can be achieved if the leaders of a church are agreed and have resolved to move forward in a particular direction. However, the failure to build both the consensus and determination for a change across the range of church leaders quickly undermines changes. Sometimes this can happen because of a lack of teaming in the group, many other times it is a lack of time, consultation and prayer.

2. *The failure to engage the rest of the church in the issues that need to be addressed.* Too often leaders might discuss an issue and come up with a proposed solution long before the wider church has even a good appreciation of the problems and challenges. The result is that they are surprised to be offered a way forward to a challenge that they did not know existed and certainly had not been able to consider.

3. *Poor planning.* Either not planning forward step by step or not defining the goal and scope of the change clearly. Sometimes this can be a failure to define clearly what is going to happen and when. At other times it will be that the change is conceptualised badly and the things that were hoped for have not been captured effectively in the vision of the change. Either way the end result is that the church ends up in a different place from where leaders hoped it would be.

4. *Communications are handled badly.* This is a consistent lesson from the Arrow leaders' feedback. Messages are too vague or general and there is too little dialogue. A real

sense of priority is not communicated. The vision is lost. People get ignored and ideas and improvements are lost along with their owners.

5. *Slow and tentative change.* In many churches a concern for how people feel about things can lead to slow, partial steps. The change gets lost in time; leaders and congregations get bored with it and all move on to the next priority before it achieves anything. A real determination is needed for major change. This can only be done over a relatively short period of time (typically one to two years). If change is given poorly defined milestones or these are put too far apart people lose track and momentum and the change gets washed away by other things.

These mirror studies in the commercial world[2] which highlight four factors as frequent causes of failure:

- A lack of senior management commitment (focus and intent).
- The failure to win hearts and minds.
- Poor planning.
- Communication failures.

Learn from your church's history

Ironically, one of the best ways to identify the most important risks is to look back at the history of the church and the changes that have been launched there. It is possible to see patterns in the history of changes in an organisation that transcend management teams and individuals and help to reveal the strengths and weaknesses of the underlying 'way we do things around here'.

The lessons can be really useful. We worked with one European manufacturing company to help them to implement a new system to improve management information and reduce the cost of doing business. History showed that previous European efforts, despite their intent, always became more complicated and expensive as they were designed. Countries and departments always succeeded in adding exceptions, or had processes that could not be changed for local reasons, or difficult changes slowed down until they were dropped. Knowing this and identifying the driving factors behind it enabled an approach to be chosen that minimised these risks – selecting carefully the local design leaders, choosing standard industry software that would not accommodate too much tweaking, and retaining a highly visible structure for governing the change succeeded in managing these risks effectively.

In your church, what has happened with previous attempts: to change the pattern of services; to launch new initiatives; to alter house groups; or to change the way decisions are made? Which worked well and which struggled? Why did they struggle?

This sort of detective work will provide a long list of factors that leaders can review. It will reveal key individuals and families. It may show which governance structures for change have worked well and which have come unstuck. If there are different centres, it will help show which tend to be more problematic and why. If there has been a schism, then the genesis and causes of the separation can be helpful in understanding how to approach changes and minimise the risk of division.

History is helpful, even where many people in a community have moved on. The persistence of patterns of behaviour and issues is explained by the cultural acclimatisation that everyone experiences when they join a group. A new member rarely significantly alters the dynamics of the group without a significant effort and a lot of disruption. The result is that, even as people in a group change, the group can quite easily retain its behavioural character.

Changes that parallel the one that the church is now considering are especially useful. These can often reveal specific risks that need to be addressed. History also shows:

- the quantity of change that the church has experienced;
- what are considered major versus minor changes; and
- the overall change history and its success or failure as perceived by the church. This will shape fear levels, cynicism and enthusiasm, depending on people's experience (within this church or others, of course).

Riverside Church – moving to multiple sites

In the early years of Riverside Church in Birmingham, after the church grew to over 100 people, a new Sunday congregation was started within a mile or so of the main meeting. This process was repeated again and again as a policy to grow a robust and mission-minded church.

However, at the point that the sixth congregation was about to start, it was felt right to all come together again. The church is now, many years later, looking at going multi-site again. There have been a number of voices that remember the time before and ask, 'Why would we do that again? It obviously failed the first time.'

Yet there are many lessons to be gleaned from the experience and although the outcomes were not what was expected it could not really be judged a failure. Actually, although running five congregations proved difficult, the church sailed through the dreaded 150-person barrier and was much bigger than it might otherwise have been when it came back together.

We may not have known it at the time but it was far more of a success than any had thought.

Use risks as signposts to shape change management

The value of considering risk, upfront and throughout the lifecycle, is in protecting and growing the change and in making sure that we put no inadvertent obstacles in the way of God's plan. We are much more likely to respond effectively to a

189

challenge knowing that it could unseat a valuable change. We will be much quicker to address issues knowing that it is important to do so for success.

After all, the reason that risk has been researched is because a whole industry has grown up (consultants, strategic advisors, investment bankers, systems-delivery houses and many others) that offers help to improve the prospects for success. A risk is highlighted to work out how to reduce it. Change brings with it different risks from the status quo and understanding what these are helps to focus the attention of leaders on the right areas.

Whatever your outlook, reviewing risk is a useful exercise to improve the way that change is handled. It does not mean doubting God's hand or direction for change. It is about following God's leading well. It is about execution not decision.

Key point summary
- We do not initiate change to succeed; we initiate change to be faithful to God's leading.
- All change carries the risk of failure – so, perhaps perversely, we need to make more changes in order to succeed more often.
- Common risks to effective change are poor planning and communications, a fractured leadership group, the failure to engage the wider church and being too tentative.
- Your own church's history of change can be a useful source of information on specific risks to watch out for through change.

14 - Address Conflict Constructively

Change provokes conflict

> 'Changes cannot be delayed until everyone
> feels comfortable with them.'
>
> *William Bridges*

We would all like people to be reasonable, to agree on the way forward and for the church to move as one when it embarks on something new. Sadly this is rarely the case. There are many reasons. We tend to pay little attention to our environment. We just carry on with what we are doing and quickly get into a relatively thoughtless routine. If you have ever commuted by car, you understand exactly how this works when you find how little memory you sometimes have of the drive to work, despite all the traffic and navigation involved. The result is that some will see the need for change whilst others will be completely oblivious to the need.

Where a church is seeking God's leading for the future and trying to discern how he is moving then we can hope that there will be a good degree of consensus about the direction. However, especially in mature and well-established congregations, there is normally a divergence of view. Indeed, in all the churches that we have ever been involved with there has not been a major change that has not left people without differences of view (even if only a few). This is to be expected even in a collaboratively developed change. The community would not reflect the diversity that God seeks in reconciling all people to himself if this wasn't the case.

One of the key roles of leaders is to seek to influence people so that they change their minds and actively support the direction that God is leading. However, an appropriate level of challenge and engagement is likely to provoke conflict at times. In this chapter we discuss:

- The fact that conflict is healthy and to be expected.
- The varied reasons why change triggers conflict and resistance.
- Principles and strategies for approaching conflict.
- The likelihood of people leaving the church.

Conflict is normal and healthy

Leaders sometimes ask if conflict is inevitable. No – but it is highly likely, even if there is no major change. Too often, behind this concern, is a view that conflict is a bad thing: something that should be absent from a united body of Christ.

This seems to be a common view in many Christian circles. There is the assumption that being Christian is being nice and conflict isn't nice. Unfortunately this approach can sometimes unleash the worst sort of passive-aggressive behaviour and avoidance tactics which are extremely unattractive and maintain superficial unity at the expense of true unity.

We need to address conflict. Freedom of choice is part of God's design for people and inevitably creates conflict.[1] There are clear disagreements in the early church.[2] Healthy relationships, in church or family or organisations, actually demand a level of conflict. Its absence would be a sign of problems: a sign that people feel too insecure or threatened to openly raise issues of difference and resolve them, or that people are not taking responsibility for their own walk with God and are overly conformist.

Addressing conflict well could be seen as a hallmark of a healthy church. It should not break the unity and peace of our relationships in Christ. It should be resolved in a fair manner, without crushing the weaker party.[3]

Unfortunately it is all too easy for real people to lose a sense of proportion, especially in the heat of emotion. So the church should prepare itself for increased conflict as it goes through change. David Brubaker's research suggests that not every type of change is as likely to generate conflict (e.g. starting a community project) and indeed some may even reduce the likelihood. But some, such as a change in the service pattern or in the decision-making structures in the church, are likely to do so. His conclusion is worth noting: 'Where there is change, there is conflict is too simple a description. Where there are insufficiently planned changes to the core meaning-making function and power relationships of the congregation, there is likely to be conflict. It may be a less memorable phrase. It seems, however, to be a more accurate conclusion.'[4]

Many reasons for conflict

Perhaps the first point to make over change-generated conflict is that people will oppose change for many different reasons. It is important that leaders begin by trying to sift these causes. John Kotter and Leonard Schlesinger[5] summarised both the different causes of resistance to change in organisations and the responses that leaders might make in addressing them. Even though they focused on commercial organisations rather than communities, they usefully highlight the issues that can provoke resistance and conflict in change. They highlight four main groups of reasons for people opposing change:

1. *Self-interest*: The change threatens something of value to them: perhaps a position of power and influence, or an activity with special meaning. In church the range is wide because of the enormously personal nature of people's

193

experience. We have seen people who became upset because change threatened a place with special memories or that was created by someone who is now dead but gave a gift to create it. We have seen the same where there has been a change in the youth ministry or music ministry that means new leaders replace existing ones. These are seen as an attack on an important role, place of influence or valued memory. People will naturally resist these.

2. *Misunderstanding*: Here people misinterpret what the change involves or its implications. They resist it for what they think it will mean not what it actually does. The creation of an informal part of the service, a shift in musical style, a new structure for welcomers or a change in the governance of the church lead people to feel that this is the 'thin end of the wedge' and will mean other changes they dislike. This is especially likely where there is a low level of trust in the congregation and a past history of badly communicated and planned change. It is easy for people to overlay unhelpful meanings on top of actions and communications that the initiators do not intend.

3. *Low tolerance to change*: Particularly where a major change is something that has been rarely experienced and people have come to expect continuity or traditional approaches. Here people find it difficult to absorb a major change for no other reason than it is something new.

4. *Genuine disagreement on the situation or solution*: People may have also looked at the issues and what needs to happen and come to a different conclusion from others. This may make them oppose a solution that they see as inappropriate or sub-optimal. They may even counter with an alternative. Buildings are a common friction point here but it can also be the same when leaders seek to rejuvenate life and mission in the church and different groups see an alternative set of issues and routes forward.

This list is not complete and describes everything in rational rather than emotional terms. Specific causes are worth highlighting, even though they sit within the four headings. For example, change can sometimes generate resistance because it breaks an unidentified community rule and seeks to redefine the way that people relate to each other, or the purpose of the church. The change might be seen as unfair but it might be difficult to get any clear answers as to why. The same might be true of a change that triggers memories or reasons deep within the stories of what originally made the church a successful community. These cultural issues can be just as significant, if difficult to uncover.

The underlying triggers can be movements in power and influence, the crossing of some cultural norm, value or belief, changes in context which impact the structures for decisions or innate differences in personality and approach between people. A change provides an excellent trigger for them to rise up and bite leaders.

Whatever the reasons, it does not necessarily mean that the only resolution is some form of compromise or coercion. It is important that leaders seek to uncover the motives behind a challenge before deciding what to do and how to approach it.

This can be difficult to do if conflict arises unexpectedly or in a heated public exchange, especially when there is a confrontation and people are ready for a fight. In these cases it is easy for bad behaviour to dominate and for sides to establish themselves quickly – leaving bystanders bewildered at what to do, leaders feeling besieged and others feeling angry and overlooked. If this happens, it is vital that leaders do not press forward with change and try to ignore the opposition. It is also important that they separate the people and the issue and try to get to a resolution of the latter. A pause with reflection and prayer is a really good first step, if necessary calling a time-out in a meeting that is going downhill and making sure that everyone understands that they are going to be heard before anything else happens.

Principles and strategies for approaching conflict

Strategy

Those who have seen the film *The Butler* will have observed two different approaches to securing civil rights in the USA in the 1960s, illustrated by the father and his son in the movie. The father works away at changing opinions by his positive, respectful and hardworking approach, building relationships which allow him to reveal his dislike of the second-class treatment of black people in the USA. His son takes a high-profile and belligerent approach that is prepared to break unjust laws and he faces imprisonment in a non-violent struggle against bigotry. His is a visible approach that confronts wrong attitudes.

Both strategies have their place, depending on the people involved, the situation and the causes of conflict. People oppose change for both bad and good reasons and this needs to shape leaders' approaches. Sometimes a strong public challenge to bad behaviour may be needed; at other times people must be won round.

Leaders need to think through how to challenge, and decide what will be most effective, both for the change and for the people involved. Sometimes it is best done in well-structured public forums, sometimes in private discussion. The strategy may need to change as the process progresses or if conflict escalates but leaders should consider the options and review their approach as things evolve.

The following are some pointers to help engagement.

Leaders' demeanour

It is vital that leaders engage with resistance in a way that reduces tensions and helps to start people on the path to resolving the conflict. This can be difficult when our own feelings and security are hurt and poor behaviour seems personally directed and aggressive.

Our approach needs to be direct to the individual, ideally face-to-face, dealing with their complaint (as opposed to any general 'people are not happy with ...'). It needs to be open and interested in listening, not immediately trying to justify the leader's position but interested in the other's views.

A calm, engaged and confident approach that expects God's truth to come to the centre of the relationship and shape the interaction is vital, as is an attitude of forgiveness for the likely harsh behaviour that will appear in the course of the conflict.

It will also help if leaders are clear about the important aspects of faith on which the church can agree and have secured a common bond with others around these. This makes the often much less important aspects of a change an area where people will recognise that differences of view can be accommodated.

Leaders need to be self-aware and remain connected

Some years ago, after a heated leaders' meeting of a wider group in the church, someone approached me and said, 'Nick, you are always so defensive. Every time someone disagrees with you, you become all spiky.' 'No, I don't!' I defensively replied ...

I thanked him and realised how hard it was for the church to make real progress with a leader who was unaware of his own emotions and responses.

Questions – non-defensive enquiry
A key starting point for leaders is to start by asking questions. These need to be asked with an open, sincere intent

and with the humility that recognises that we each only have a part of the truth and can learn from others. The objective is to find out honest answers from those who are upset and to be seen to value the answers whatever they may be.

In itself, this can be a powerful intervention. It is vital to find out who is really upset and why they feel this way – directly. Then after getting an answer to the first 'why' it is vital to ask why again, to find out the real, deeper reasons for conflict. For instance, in one reordering project an arch critic of the work was a lady, who it emerged, opposed the project primarily out of loyalty to her now dead husband who had disliked it, not because she disliked it.

Leaders also need a real sense for when an issue is not just an external issue but is challenging someone's identity (even their own). When something triggers an attack on our identity, it can quickly trigger an emotionally driven response that is out of proportion to the issue. When this happens, people need space to reflect, and support for their pain.

Open reflection and interpretation

Open engagement and questions, if done well, can start to move resolution closer by triggering reflection on all sides of the quarrel: reflection on each side's actions and real motives; reflection on the change and whether it really means what it has been interpreted to mean; and reflection on options to open the dialogue up and understand what others are feeling.

This process of reflecting and then interpreting behaviour and apparent reasoning, especially when done with a generous spirit that seeks to sit in the other person's shoes, can start to unlock conflict and de-escalate it. It is why leaders need to lean into conflict not away from it and engage it constructively. It can be the route to understanding.

If there is a real desire to hear what others think and why, it helps reduce the tension that often makes these interactions so emotional and unpleasant. It also creates options. It can reveal how context (tops, middles, bottoms – Chapter 10) is driving the conflict: people's roles; how decisions are made; the information to hand – these all shape behaviour, perhaps more than we like to think. Leaders should be aware of the power structures (formal and informal) in the church and watch out for movements in these and the way this shapes behaviour.

Reflect on the end outcome

Asking people to think through what they really want as an outcome can also help. Outcomes can often be much more complementary than people initially think they will be. People begin to see what they might want now, as opposed to the hurt from what they have lost. They begin to change their views as they see the undesirable results of opposition without any positive goal.

Avoid labels

Throughout the process of conflict it is easy to put labels on people and behaviour. Labels are shorthand but all too frequently they conceal rather than illuminate what is really going on and they can quickly start to suggest bigger gaps and obstacles between people than really exist. It is important that leaders do not use these to summarise the attitudes and actions of one group or person either to themselves or others.

The more this can be avoided, the more real reflection and understanding will be built. It helps to avoid the leaders filling in the details between someone's behaviour and their motives or attitudes and reasons. Instead it invites more questions to build understanding.

Call out conflict as the issue?

At some point leaders need to decide the extent to which the conflict can be addressed as the change is progressed or whether it needs highlighting and addressing specifically and separately from the change. The latter approach is probably essential when relationships have broken down or friction is becoming destructive to the individuals or the community.

Conflict can derail change and even a church. How bad is bad?

Speed Leas, a consultant with the Alban Institute in the US, has provided a helpful outline to help churches weigh up how serious the conflict is. He describes five levels with increasing intensity and impact. Towards the higher levels of this ladder it can be useful to have a third party, acceptable to all sides, to intervene. Around the middle level it might require special meetings, maybe even with a facilitator or mediator from within the church. Towards the bottom it needs the use of basic interaction tools to try to unlock and address the problems. If things start to escalate, leaders need to address conflict itself, separately from the change.

- Level 1: *Problems to solve.* Normal and healthy with easy communications focused on the problem not the people.
- Level 2: *Disagreement.* Here people guard their position a bit more, withholding information and protecting themselves. The problem that needs resolution has started to move into the background.
- Level 3: *Contest.* People see conflict with winners and losers. Emotions and attacks with distorted communications start to make this a difficult level to deal with.
- Level 4: *Fight or flight.* Here people are starting to want to get rid of their opponents. There are factions and blame being attached to people. The position seems to be stuck.

- Level 5: *Intractable*. This is the 'Holy War' level where principles are at stake and the means are totally lost beneath the goals. Condemnation dominates, with overt fighting, and issues are long since submerged under vitriolic and destructive behaviour.

If the situation is well into level 3, especially if it is still getting worse, then there is a serious issue that probably is now starting to overshadow any thoughts of the change and needs urgent resolution. Dealing with resistance quietly and privately, with gentle persuasion, may well work at the lower levels of conflict but it will not work if things rise to level 3.

Priorities

If there are many individuals who are unhappy, then especially with a small leadership group it can be important to prioritise who to deal with first or where to spend a limited amount of time. It can help in these circumstances to list all the people who need to be covered and place them on a circle with the proximity to the centre of the circle being determined by how important their commitment is to the implementation of the change.

The aim would be to work on the issues from the centre outwards. This can be overlaid by a view on the likelihood of securing a positive outcome and this weighting can be used to modify the order in which the leaders work on the people.

General approaches

More generally, Kotter and Schlesinger identify six strategies to address resistance. Not all of them are equally attractive but they do cover the breadth of options effectively. They suggest that once leaders have understood the drivers for resistance they should adopt one or more of the following approaches:

1. *Educate and communicate*: This helps especially if there is misunderstanding or uncertainty behind the resistance. Good communication (clear, timely, focused, open and two-way) is a powerful lever to defuse tension and problems. It is most effective when specifically targeted to the right people and their concerns. The need is to make sure that everyone is clear about the facts – the what, when, why and who is involved. Helping people to really understand what it means for them may help address some challenges.

2. *Involve*: The second strategy is to build participation and involvement. This is a vital part of leading in a church context. If there has been little involvement by the time the change is defined, it is difficult to go back and rebuild it but it should still be done. Leaders can only apologise and try to build engagement properly. It is sometimes possible. Involvement helps relieve resistance. It is also important for getting to the best shape of the change. Rarely do leaders have all the information and insights that enable change to be scoped optimally.

3. *Support and facilitate*: This can be a vital way of helping people when their capacity for change is low or when there is a misunderstanding. It can build confidence in the likelihood of success. It strengthens resolve and reduces fear. It will not address self-interested resistance or different assessments of the need for change directly but it can help.

4. *Incentivise*: This is about negotiating with those resisting a change to find some way to compensate for their losses. We deal with it in more detail below.

The final two strategies are the least attractive of the ones identified by the authors and should be pursued carefully. They may reflect an ill-considered change or an overdue change but to an extent they are an inevitable part of important change because not everyone will finally agree.

5. *Push ahead regardless*: In some extreme circumstances this may be the best or only course of action. Sometimes people dig in and will not move. This can be a way forward, where: a vocal group have decided that they are opposed to what is happening despite a different sense of God's leading in the main body of the church and leadership; or people are trying to block a change unreasonably. However, leaders need to bring the change before God and check that they have approached it in a good way. It can then be appropriate to push ahead but it should be done retaining a desire to see those in opposition to the change still moving forward with God, in fellowship with others (ideally in the church) and in good relations with people.

6. *Marginalise or ignore*: As with the previous strategy, this is less than ideal and should be adopted as a last resort. It can lead to the resistor leaving the church but nonetheless this can sometimes be the best outcome for all. Often the personal motivations for someone resolutely opposing a change or hounding a leadership group can be poor. Ignoring people or deliberately marginalising them is a hard strategy but once other options have been pursued it can be the only way forward.

These are strategies. They identify a good range of choices that leaders have in addressing conflict and resistance. They do not address how the strategy is pursued. Leaders need wisdom for both.

Incentives and losses

People often resort to conflict when faced with change because they feel they are losing something. Sometimes they can be compensated by finding out 'what might we give back to compensate for what we have taken away?' as William Bridges puts it. In a work situation this might mean paying more or offering better terms and conditions but we have not been in many churches where these incentives exist, at least for the majority of the congregation.

However, incentives are worth thinking about. The starting point for this is to work out what it is that individuals or groups are losing and to identify the most significant aspects:

- Involvement and a clear role
- Status or influence
- Key friendships or a venue for these
- A group identity
- An enjoyable and fulfilling activity
- A cherished memory or place
- A sense of belonging or importance
- Security

These are just a few of the potential losses that people feel and that might sit behind arguments and fuel resistance. Finding a creative way to compensate for their loss can produce surprising results.

In one business meeting that we were facilitating, the most senior client, an experienced and successful partner in an accounting practice, began to disengage as the team worked towards defining a strategy to go forward. It was clear that he felt his status was being undermined by the effective working of the team. The resolution of this challenge was to put him right back in the centre of the group with a simple device – control of a bell to chair the individual feedback. This was a small but powerful way of addressing his felt loss of status.

At a church where one of the wardens of the church was stepping down after many years, the post of church administrator was created. This addressed two issues at once. It immediately gave this person another clear role that enabled them to continue to energetically serve God in the church and so stay fully engaged. It also helped to address the potential for administrative weaknesses in the governance of the church and ensure that many of the important day-to-day tasks were effectively parcelled out across the congregation.

In another setting where a change in service patterns meant that the choir was losing the opportunity to minister in one service, their role in one of the other services was strengthened. This helped the choir members to see that their role was not merely being rejected but repositioned.

These sorts of actions can be of great importance. They are kind and they demonstrate leaders reaching out to people in change. Such kindness helps to legitimise change. In this way it also lubricates the wheels for further change as it shows that each person matters even in a change.

The likelihood of people leaving

Pastorally hearted leaders are always concerned that people might leave the congregation. They feel the hurt. There is a sense amongst some leaders that, 'If people leave it is my responsibility and I have done something badly.'

The reality is that in a major change it is almost certain that some people will leave. Some will leave physically and loudly, some will withdraw from activities and roles quietly but the net impact is the same. They have been lost, at least for a while. Many of these will leave with accusations that they were not listened to or their contribution was ignored. Some will feel angry. Some will be sure that the church is going in the wrong direction and they have made the right decision to leave and go elsewhere.

As Sir Laurence Olivier once said, 'No matter how well you perform there's always somebody of intelligent opinion who thinks it's lousy.'

There is almost no change in which everyone is happy and engaged. People will leave with all manner of emotions and with all sorts of reasons. It is one of the implications of the diffusion curve: the laggards are those who will not adopt a change until forced. It is always sad when this happens but it will happen.

> **No important change without pain and loss**
>
> In discussing the pastoral challenge of change we have sometimes asked leaders to reflect back on their own experience of significant church change and ask if there has ever been one that has taken place without someone failing to accept it and so withdrawing or even leaving the community.
>
> In all cases where people have reflected on major changes they have always been able to identify at least one person who left. Sometimes this can be close to people leading the change. In one case, it was the partner of one of the people responsible for instituting changes in the worship styles.

Leaders do not lead for the majority, nor do they have to be at the leading edge of changes and ideas but if they are following God's leading then they will need to lead their church through many changes – changes in the local environment and catchment, changes in the shape and character of the congregation and changes in the way that God is leading. At each of these points, the changes being made will be 'major' for some people and they will not want to change.

It is one reason why rooting people's identity and security in Christ is so important.

Sometimes we can be surprised. One of the most encouraging stories that we heard was from a minister brought into an ageing Baptist church with a missional heart. After twelve months or so the minister brought forward proposals to change many aspects of the services and the ministry. It was difficult for the elderly members of the church. They struggled to relate to the modern services and methods. The minister related how he met a number of the elders who explained the trouble that they were having. However, they said that although they might not seem to be behind the changes, they recognised the importance of what was happening. They were confident that this was God's direction and they encouraged him to continue with their every blessing. He recognised that they had given up a lot for the change and although they might never be able to fully adapt to the new way of worship he knew that they were entirely supportive.

Sometimes it is not possible to please everyone

One church experienced schism despite the strenuous efforts of leaders to prevent it.

Revival began in the otherwise traditional congregation with an influx of new Christians following a mission. These new joiners were much younger and with no commitment to the traditional services.

Despite steady changes in the approach to church, both modernisers and traditionalists became restive, one group with the slow pace of change, the other with erosion of the past ways of doing things. Although some traditionalists left as change continued, the tensions increased, especially around the fundamentals of services. Eventually, and despite work by the overall leader, there was a full-scale split.

The modernisers left to set up a separate fellowship, leaving what remained of the traditionalists and the more moderate elements in the original church.

However, the story is not entirely a sorry one. The minister was unwilling to let the split remain a sore and continued to reach out to those who had left. Such was the strength of this exercise of love that the two communities ended up partnering in ministry despite their differences, and ill-feeling was quickly dispersed.

The leadership team need to be clear about the importance of the change in the life of the church and of God's leading. A planned and stepped process needs to be followed. People need to be engaged throughout the change and a way to meet their needs sought. Yet conflict is likely and should not be avoided.

Conversations become important vehicles to encourage, retain and affirm people. However, people make their own decisions and sometimes that will mean they decide to leave. One large church that went through an extensive and well-planned consultative process to modify the service pattern still lost people who, in the end, would or could not accept the changes to the role that the choir was playing in some of these services. It was not many people. There was no fall-out in the church. The loss only saddened people, but there was still loss.

Key point summary
- Change is likely to provoke conflict. Not everyone will agree.
- Conflict is not bad. It is healthy. The key is to handle it well.
- Resistance is natural, normal and healthy. Leaders should understand why it is happening before deciding how to handle it.
- Resistance can be handled by education and communication, involvement, support or incentives, and sometimes by pushing ahead regardless.
- Leaders need to be adept at identifying and handling people's losses from change to help the process work more smoothly.
- In conflict situations, leaders' attitude and behaviour is critical. It helps to:
  - remain calm, open and engaged even in the face of personal criticism;
  - ask questions to get to the roots of the issues;
  - decide if conflict needs to be called out and addressed directly;
  - call people to work out what they really want; and
  - avoid labelling people (either explicitly or implicitly).
- In bad situations, leaders will need to prioritise with whom and how they handle conflict.

- Effective change will often alienate some people. This can be unavoidable. It is not necessarily a bad thing for the church or the person.

15 - Create and Sustain Momentum

Change can be derailed even after a successful launch. A change is not realised until transition is complete. This can take a long time and it is vital that leaders create enough momentum to get to the end of the journey. In this chapter we look at how to create and sustain momentum through change:

- The defining character of success.
- Securing quick wins.
- Adaption.
- Measuring progress.

The defining character of success

Although there is limited research on how to sustain a change, Buchanan et al.[1] have studied this and concluded that persistence depends on three dimensions:

1. *Substance.* Is it a real change of great importance to the community? Then it is most likely to persist. People will recognise it as still needing energy to ensure it works and leaders will keep it high on their priority list from one year to the next so that it does not disappear like the latest fashion.

2. *The implementation process.* Well-executed change unsurprisingly lasts longer and has more impact than poorly implemented change. Execution is really important for any innovation if it is to survive, as the natural forces of inertia seek to pull the community back to its old shape and behaviour. Using the disciplines highlighted in Chapter 12 is a vital tool for creating and sustaining a change.

3. *Time and pace.* Change has to be given long enough to work through. Rushing it doesn't work. Neither does tiptoeing slowly forward. Often, at the start, leaders underestimate the time needed, or more particularly underestimate the energy and resources needed for a major change.

We are often asked if it is better to change things quickly or slowly. Unsurprisingly, there is no right answer to this question. All other things being equal, faster is better than slower so that the discomfort that surrounds the dead zone is minimised (bearing in mind though that people do not necessarily transition quickly). This retains focus. Certainly, where changes are stepped and strung out, there can be problems in trying to maintain momentum. Old issues tend to keep being raised because of the reminders of the past and a slow speed often suggests tentativeness rather than firmness of purpose.

However, the critical thing is to choose an appropriate speed for the real aspects of the change (technical and behavioural) and then put in the additional effort and resource that is required to help people move forward.

Secure quick wins

People do not like the dead zone of transition and do not like moving into it as they go into a change. This makes the early stages of a change important for creating momentum. It should be a time for encouragement and the demonstration of progress. The first few meetings of a new governance structure or new service times and formats are important validations of the change and its value.

It helps to find opportunities for what consultants call 'quick wins' (sadly, they are rarely as quick and easy as they sound). These are events, experiences or demonstrations of the benefits of the change. They can be planned in some cases or sought out in others. They might be people's testimony of the value of the new, a problem avoided by the new way of doing things, the use of a new service to invite someone special to come in and speak.

Planning for the new needs to be well-executed (even better than the old) and extra thought must be put into the finishing touches that demonstrate care. This helps to encourage those who are feeling uncomfortable with the move into the unknown.

Another aspect of this type of encouragement is for leaders to mark progress with suitable celebrations: celebrations of things that are being put aside but which God has used in the past, or celebrations of new successes as things progress. It is easy for leaders to become too serious or task-focused in a period of major change. Joy and celebration are really helpful. They lift spirits and help everyone appreciate the value of moving forward together. It can sometimes be helpful to make sure that one person has responsibility for looking for opportunities to do this so that it does not get forgotten. This needs to be someone who has a good eye for celebration and it needs to be done with sincerity when there is something to celebrate.

A second area to consider is that of change capacity. In our experience many leadership groups struggle with this. They underestimate how much energy it drains out of people to adjust to change. As a result they struggle to whittle down the church 'to do' list. Despite everyone's best efforts, there is only so much time and resource and some things will not happen on any long list of 'essential' items. It is far better and easier if the list is winnowed ahead of time and a few priorities are chosen and then implemented whilst the others are postponed or dropped. Things go faster and people feel the speed and energy. Leaders do not get as tired.

It is important to remember, when compiling the list, that it needs to embrace all the other items that the team have on their agenda as priorities, not just the change. These use leadership time and church energy and need to be factored in.

Adapt

Leaders can feel that they are fighting a deadweight of inertia in some churches. The tendency in these circumstances can be that, once a change is underway, especially if it has traction, leaders are reluctant to tamper with it in case it allows people to recreate the past in a new way by changing the change.

Nonetheless, it is unwise to create a new dogma out of an innovation and to prevent the incorporation of improvements or refinements that people suggest, and are in keeping with the way forward. It is vital that leaders do not freeze out ideas in efforts to stop backsliding because the sensitivity and agility that comes with change is one of its benefits. It helps to keep the church in step with the Spirit. This demands that good new ideas are incorporated and allowed to flourish.

Leaders must encourage the congregation to keep on contributing ideas and improvements, especially if the change has already leveraged people's participation and contribution from the start. It is inconsistent to build change within the life of a community and then to stop contributions once the change is underway.

Even though there is evidence that organisations tend to go through periods of quasi-stationery equilibrium and then other periods of rapid change, it remains vital that leaders keep looking forward and assuming that God will continue to lead the church into more innovations and not fewer. Whenever it launches a major change the church is going down a path of exploration. Change itself needs to change as people understand better what needs to be done. This applies to leaders just as much as to members.

Measure progress

We have said little about measuring progress through change. Yet this can be a really helpful tool for maintaining momentum. It is life-giving to have feedback. It keeps a change grounded and helps to ensure the church achieves its goals.

In some cases formal metrics might seem to add little. Well-connected leaders who are open to feedback are unlikely to find new news in complicated measures. They will have their antennas up and quickly identify how things are going and what needs to be improved or changed. They will be able to sense where the people are in their feeling and thinking, how well they are transitioning and what the impact of the change is on the community and its environment.

Nonetheless, our experience is that the same people who do this are always interested in measures as well. These are additional sources of insight and feedback. Enthusiastic leaders will typically try to add other information to informal discussion. Metrics are not always the ABC of church numbers (attendees, buildings and collections). They can be derived from surveys, structured group feedback or structured 1:1 discussions.

A desire to measure progress, especially if it is built on clear aims for the change, provides the easiest way for leaders to discern that a change has run its course and can be considered complete.

Knowing when a change is complete can be relatively straightforward when it is a tangible project (e.g. a reordering or building), although even here, if the outcomes desired are more than only better surroundings for the church, the metrics should go beyond the last lick of paint on the chancel wall into real human outcomes.

However, change is often a much more nuanced exercise. If it is a change in the style of worship in services, a more disciplined walk with God, a more missional approach for individuals and church, then the goals are much more difficult to translate into measures. Change is more about attitude and behaviour. It requires a little more thought and creativity.

Most changes of a qualitative nature will end by being superseded by the next change. The outcomes sought may have not been fully realised but need reinvigorating. Sometimes they have been realised but it is time to move on to the next challenge. This is fine but it is helpful if leaders can state that a change has ended and what has been achieved, so that there remains real clarity and unanimity within the leadership group. If this clarity is lost it is easy for people to perceive differing priorities in the church and some members will continue to focus on tasks that are no longer the priority.

One of the key lessons from business is that it is actually a lot harder to get a project or change stopped than started. Ending changes cleanly helps to address this and prevents a feeling of an overload of change that is entirely unnecessary.

This chapter focuses on the disciplines and challenges of pressing changes home in the life of the church and not letting them peter out with little lasting impact. The real benefits of launching change are only realised if they land well. In far too many cases these are lost because the leadership effort and attention that is needed to finish well is not given.

We must look to complete the tower. If the change is really important and the outcomes are worth pursuing then this should be straightforward because all eyes will be on the prizes and not on the specific machinations of the change.

Key point summary

- Sustained change depends on its substance, effective execution and persistence through time.
- Momentum can be helped by identifying and securing 'quick wins'.
- Momentum can also be maintained by measuring progress. This is a really useful and often neglected discipline.
- Often, change itself needs to adapt for it to be sustained.

16 - A Word about Cultural Change

The church is not the only organisation that is concerned about its culture. Most leaders at some point seem to become concerned about the fit between their organisational culture and its purpose. A 2013 culture and change survey conducted globally by Strategy& highlights this[1]:

- 84% of leaders think culture is critical to business success, but
- 51% believe their current culture needs a significant overhaul and
- only 54% believe that their current culture supports sustainable change

It seems that, as the West has become more anxious and less trusting over recent years, the topic of cultural change has become more prominent. It is as if leaders are recognising that their job is becoming difficult and that the issues they are facing are increasingly driven by a wider set of people issues.

Church leaders seemed equally concerned. We have been asked many times if the approaches we outline are appropriate for culture change. Much of what we suggest does indeed address aspects of culture. However, it is worth considering the topic of culture specifically to address:

- What is culture such that a leader might want to change it?
- How practical is it to change culture directly?
- What are the principal ways in which leaders might think about addressing cultural issues?

Culture defined

What is culture? Typically, in the search for a definition we end up with expressions like 'the way we do things around here', patterns of behaviour, values that are expressed, rules for getting on in the organisation and beliefs about the way the world works. All speak to aspects of culture. However, one of the world's foremost experts on culture, Edgar Schein, says that although these topics reflect an organisation's culture, culture has several levels that constitute artefacts, espoused values and underlying assumptions. He defines the essence of culture as: 'A pattern of basic assumptions and beliefs that are shared by members of an organisation, operate unconsciously and define an organisation's view of itself and its environment.'[2] This definition emphasises:

- Culture is the property of a social unit. Where there is no shared social identity there is no culture.
- It is created by sufficient common experiences in addressing internal and external challenges that the unit builds a shared view of the world, how it works and how best to approach it. It is fundamental. The worldview then shapes values and in turn behaviours.
- This worldview can change over time, albeit slowly, as there is new shared learning.

This helps to explain why it is so difficult to address culture. Essentially we are looking at habits and beliefs, both of which are deeply rooted. It is difficult to identify and explain what our own largely unconscious assumptions are, let alone identify this for a group. Even people coming from outside a group, who may be able to see the artefacts of culture, might find it difficult to describe accurately what sits beneath these.

However, Schein's definition also explains why it is so significant. The way that we see the world shapes everything that

218

we do, from where we put emphasis to how we go about doing things.

Is culture change practical?

Succinct definition doesn't necessarily help in the quest to change culture. We are wary of setting cultural change as a goal and we are not alone. Something as all-encompassing and intangible makes it difficult to address. Even setting it as a goal might be counterproductive. A recent article in *Forbes* suggested that the best way to change culture was to stop talking about it.[3] Similarly, emeritus professor of management at Wharton, Larry Hrebiniak says, 'To fix culture, don't focus on culture because there are so many other variables involved.'[4] Culture is so broad. It is something that supports all the activity of the church and yet is also shaped by every activity. This makes it tough to change and easy to get lost in.

Some strategic advisors suggest that it is best not to target culture at all. So some say things like: 'Culture does not change because we desire to change it. Culture changes when the organisation is transformed; the culture reflects the realities of people working together every day.'[5] Others, even heavily into cultural issues, such as Jon Katzenbach, caution leaders to treat the prevailing culture as the background to work within, rather than something that can be targeted for wholesale change.

Similar advice can be inferred from those who emphasise the importance of reaching back into community history to find values or attitudes in the past which have relevance for the present. Our suggestions are:

- Actions which seem to cut across broad cultural issues are unlikely to succeed. They are too complex to justify and execute and are undermined by the culture. It is better to be specific about changes and target these. Attention should be focused on a few critical behaviours and their drivers.

- Where possible, a good starting point is to identify one or two positive attributes of the current culture. Honour these recognised strengths and use them to leverage against cultural weaknesses or obstacles to change.
- Use 'critical incidents' (examples of positive actions or negative outcomes from specific events) to promote the learning of better behaviours or viewpoints or to challenge assumptions and help people to develop new ways to solve problems. In doing this lessons will only be absorbed if taught repeatedly.
- Cultural change is best approached indirectly rather than directly. Don't talk about cultural change or the need to change values. It is better to talk in terms of changes to specific habits and beliefs, or focus on specific aspects of the church that can demonstrate the new views and values at work and then promote reflection on the lessons and possible extensions.
- Leaders should be wary of confusing climate with culture. Climate is much more temporary and can set the tone, mood and feeling of a place but can often be changed quite quickly by addressing specific causes.

Actions to create culture change

Much of what we have already discussed in terms of approach and examples applies to culture. Indeed, our points about the soft side of vision have a particular resonance in this area. However, some interventions are particularly relevant when targeting habits and beliefs. These comprise leaders' behaviour, learning opportunities and organisational levers.

Leaders' presence and actions

The strongest impact that we can have on culture is to address our own behaviour. Culture is built up by previous leaders' behaviour. Their approach and attitudes shape the way a community sees the world. Therefore, unsurprisingly, the starting point needs to be the way that the leaders themselves see the world and portray this to the rest of the church. To help the community look at new problems and different solutions, it is necessary for leaders' own views to change.

This is why in bigger organisations leaders start change efforts with the extended group of leaders and the way that they see the opportunities and challenges of the organisation (see Chapter 10 on the Joshua Group). In 1990s' New York, the Police Commissioner, Bill Bratton, took all his leaders onto the subway day and night so that they began to understand why citizens called it the 'electric sewer' and were scared to use it. One incoming chief executive of Campbell's held his first board meeting in the back room of a retail store and at one point in the agenda led his executives to meet bemused shoppers in the soup aisle. Some retailers ensure that their leaders regularly work on the tills. Some service organisations require managers to spend time answering the phones. This helps them to see the world in a new way (typically as customers and frontline staff see it). Once we see the world differently and relevantly then we can shape how others in the organisation see it. Leaders shape community culture through many personal actions:

- By our example, we offer a role model of appropriate words and actions (e.g. starting on time, involving people in decisions, planning activities and events properly, delivering against promised action, not avoiding conflict, caring for people, etc.).
- By where we focus our attention and praise, we signal what are the important issues and priorities and what behaviour is good or bad.

- By whom we appoint, whether to paid or volunteer positions, we are seen to approve some people and not others and so appointees become exemplars of good behaviour.
- By our standards and expectations, we can influence directly. If we hold ourselves to high standards and expect others to adopt high standards this shapes the culture.
- By our agenda, perceived both in what we say but more particularly by what we do and where and how we spend our time.
- By our reaction to crises, both what is seen as a crisis and by how we respond emotionally and practically.

Learning experiences

Culture is shaped by the almost unconscious learning that occurs when we mix with others. Through this we learn what is acceptable, what is not, what is seen to work and what is important. However, leaders can seek to help the church learn new habits and beliefs by designing experiences and enabling people to reflect on them. This covers a wide variety of possible methods, for instance:

- We can educate. If the issue is the church welcome, we can organise teaching on hospitality, where people can reflect on when they felt welcomed/unwelcome and why (e.g. in shops, leisure facilities, or when visiting churches), or even see if members have access to businesses which train staff on service and can open their doors to a benchmark visit.
- We can arrange visits to other churches to see how they approach particular activities, worship, outreach, etc. and learning what works and others' perspectives.
- Look afresh at the measures by which we judge how well things are going (e.g. attendance at specific services, numbers in home groups, giving per head, enjoyment

levels in services, levels of participation by different demographics, geographies).

- Organise for practical skills training (e.g. conflict resolution, Bible reading, counselling, biblical knowledge, customer service).
- Teach from the Bible on key topics that need to change.

Whatever is done, it is important to remember that a one-off intervention is unlikely to succeed. Strong cultures are resistant to short-term modification. People need repeated exposure to lessons if they are really to start to see the world differently. Leaders will often need to think of many different ways to help people to learn new beliefs if they want the change to really stick.

Organisational levers

There are parts of the church's life which can be particularly important in shaping habits and beliefs if used wisely and consistently:

- Formal and informal communications: The content, focus and presentation of news sheets, announcements, courses, the church magazine, etc. can help focus church attention on important areas. The activities highlighted or featured more or less heavily in notices and comments have the same impact.
- Feedback and measures: How success is judged and how much attention is paid to learning from what is being done especially in a non-judgmental and positive way. Increasing the amount and use of feedback can be a powerful way of opening people's eyes to new truths.
- Espoused values and stories: What is said is important, in particular about why things are being done and what behaviours are acceptable or unacceptable. It becomes much more impactful when it is consistent through time

223

and against actions. The illustrations or experiences shared, publicly honouring positive behaviour, and confronting toxic attitudes (privately and publicly) are powerful.

- Power structures: Church decision-making processes and structures also shape culture. Altering these structures or moving people where these conflict with important parts of the mission or desired culture of the church can help.

- Facilities and core processes (e.g. welcome, coffee and social time, service participation, away-days, study and sermon series): We often forget how powerfully the day-to-day way things are done shapes how we perceive things. Our welcome can be bad simply because it is badly organised not because people want to be unwelcoming. The building can be cold, dowdy or leave people unable to see or hear. No one may be taking responsibility for it. There may be no social time. Similarly, if more people actively participate in church life, the more it is clear people are expected to use their gifts for others.

Culture change, or perhaps better, cultural development, is a complex and important topic in its own right and we have only been able to touch on some of the most significant aspects of it in this chapter.

If leaders sense a need for change in this area, then accurate and specific diagnosis of why, and in what specific ways, change is needed is vital. Being focused pays great dividends and enables leaders to use the three types of intervention that we describe to maximum effect either as part of a wider change or on their own.

Key point summary

- Explicit cultural change is a difficult and risky task. It depends on helping people to learn new ways of seeing familiar tasks, challenges and purposes.
- It is advisable:
  - For change to be highly targeted in this area.
  - To leverage values that the culture respects to generate change.
  - To tackle the issue indirectly.
  - To focus on 'critical incidents' as learning opportunities.
- The leaders' presence and actions are critical. However, this can be augmented by using much of what already is done to generate new learning opportunities.
-

17 - Summary: Organising for Change

This chapter seeks to draw together the various threads that have been explored throughout the book and provide a guide to bringing all the different aspects of handling change into one place.

It is not possible for us to provide a definitive, specific map for changes. If it was, we are sure someone would have provided this long ago. The route that your own church must take will depend on so many factors that the permutations would leave the average GPS navigation aid with serious problems. It all depends: on the nature of the change; the starting point and history of change in the church; the different perspectives, issues and groups in the church community; the nature and strength of the leadership team; the nature of the crisis that needs to be addressed ... and myriad other things.

This chapter will not provide a route map but a framework that draws together the threads covered in the book. It is the closest we get to a methodology on a topic that does not yield itself readily to one. It will help to position the messages that you have found in each chapter into a more rounded whole. We cover:

- Where do we start?
- Navigation.
- What do we need to look after?
- A four-step framework.
- Good to go?

Where do we start?

Foundations

There are inevitably several different starting points for making use of the learning in this book. It is heavily influenced by when the book is being consulted. Is it before anything has been done? Is the church in the middle of change and something is not going so well? Are people clear what change is needed? Do you know why your church exists?

Regardless of where in the process of change you are starting from, the first thing must be to start to gain some sense of what God is doing in your situation, area and community. Change in church is about seeking to remain in, and support, the work that God wants to do where you are. All the better if this can be done with all the other leaders in the church and in a way that allows plenty of time for God to speak into the situation and the way forward. Even without this it is worth creating the space to allow him to speak. The starting point is 'Why – why are we here as the worshipping community of God?'

The priority is to start to ask questions. Questions are amongst the most powerful tools available to people and knowing the right ones to ask of God, yourself and others is the only way to begin to work out the way forward. They are needed to build up a picture of what the current situation is really like and what it could and should be like. They open up a gap – the two end points of the journey of change. Some people feel you need to start with one rather than the other but the truth is that you need both because without these you have no bearing to follow and no understanding of the most important things that need to change.

Ironically, as we say in Chapter 6, the foremost question to answer is Why? rather than Where? It is foundational.

Understanding the 'why' for the church is a powerful way of becoming much clearer about the real state of things and the direction that the church needs to go in. The 'why' then drives a lot of the framing of the information that can be uncovered with other questions.

Perhaps the 'how', which is always one that comes up quite high on our own agendas, is the least relevant at this stage. The story of the design of the Sydney Opera House, one of the world's most iconic buildings and busiest arts complexes, illustrates this well. Legend has it that Jorn Utzon, the Danish architect who produced the design, drew it in crayon on a piece of paper and that it was only selected after being rescued from the reject pile by a late-arriving Finnish-American architect on the judging panel. At selection no one knew how to construct the giant trademark shells that everyone recognises. The 'how' was worked out, somewhat painfully, through the1960s by architect, engineers and suppliers.

Start with 'why' – even if you are in the middle of change.

Building the support structures

There are then some foundations for handling change well that tend to be important regardless of where you are in the process. It can be worth digging down to put these in place even if things will take a little longer to progress or you are in the middle of a bit of a storm. These building blocks are:

- To be clear where you are (as one or more individuals). How resilient and how well are you? Are the supports that you need in place to enable this change to proceed? It is important to identify issues that are going to cloud (or are already doing so) the necessary change and that need to be resolved before going further, if they can be.
- To develop a clear, engaged and coherent leadership team that is up to the change. In some circumstances this might

even mean up to leading the church. Putting the necessary leadership in place is vital. It will help a leader who is struggling but it will undoubtedly slow things down and open the change up to challenge from others who are brought into the team. This may still be the best first step.

- To consider the strength of relationships in the church and its commitment to following God and being an intentional church. Sometimes a smaller specific change can be a distraction from what the church needs to do to address vital aspects of its life together. The change can need to be at the 'living out church' level rather than the 'change the service format' level. Leaders should not be afraid of stepping back where necessary, especially if the 'why' is unclear.
- To become clear of the 'brutal facts' (as Jim Collins describes them)[1] of the present position, rather than accept at face value what is too often a mistaken view of where the church is on any topic. This can clearly flow from questions but it can also mean some painful digging to uncover the reality rather than perceptions.

Stop and reconsider

If you are consulting this book in the middle of a change, especially where things are not going well then it is worth considering whether it is time to stop the change.

This can be helpful, especially if the foundations are not in place. It can mean stopping the change permanently or temporarily and it can involve winding it back (if that is possible).

It can enable a change to be rethought or it can provide time to put important foundations in place before either proceeding or rethinking. If things are proceeding but it looks likely that it is not going to work out well and there are several foundations missing then this may well be the best course of action possible. It is too easy to think that we must finish because we have started, even if we are going to finish badly. That is not true.

This book focuses on handling the change rather than on the nature of the change. However, if you are looking at this when reconsidering a broader change (or even before embarking on one) then you may find the leaders' landscape in the Appendix useful as a prompt list of the sort of elements that you might build into any consideration when reviewing the need for change and searching out where God might be leading.

Navigation

Where in the process is everyone
The next most important step is to identify where everyone is in the process of change. This means not just understanding the position on the external change. It is just as important to gain a sense of where all the different groups of people in church are who need to transition successfully for the change to 'work'.

This second task can only be done by talking with people and identifying what they are feeling and how they are responding (see the chart in Chapter 4 on spotting the emotions). In doing so, leaders can gain a sense of what issues are still there. The list of factors driving tension and resistance or enthusiasm and encouragement can be useful to identify the next practical steps to take.

This thinking should then enable you to use the four-step process, described later, to work out what how to move forward, put more structure around the change, or backfill on elements that have so far been overlooked. The process is a great aid to navigation. It clearly works most easily if you are trying to use it when all is calm but you sense a change may be needed. However, if you are in the middle of a change and things are not going well, it can still be valuable to structure thinking and as a gauge of where you are and what actions might be appropriate.

Immediate agenda

Wherever you find yourself in the process of change it will be important to:

- Do an inventory of what is in place and what is missing (see next section) to identify gaps and if and how these should be filled.
- Work up an accurate view of what the issues and risks are, which of them might be materialising and how each of them can be handled in priority order.
- Work at the issues in a group – where possible not just on your own – and pray, debate and discuss the things that need to be done.

The immediate priority is for things to be under control. There is a personal emotional need that drives this desire. It is also important because it makes it possible for leaders to focus on what needs to be done to influence the situation. However, it is vital that this does not result in an authoritarian and isolating intervention that is taken to pull things in for defensive reasons. This will do more damage than good. Rather, control is about information: becoming clear about where you are, who is doing what, what is working and what is not, and where the gaps and issues are. It is about gathering people and programmes together to help get the church and its leaders back into a position of influence over events. This, then, is a platform for effective leadership in church.

What do we need to look after?

Whatever type of change is being undertaken there are a number of common areas that will need to be considered and addressed, if the change is to run smoothly (or as smoothly as is possible). These are to be found in the change landscape (in the

Appendix – middle of the chart) but in summary form they are listed below and have been covered through the book:

Elements that must be covered

People	Rationale	Activities and plans
Me wellness and resilience	A clear need for change The church why The change why & church readiness	Governance how will the change be organised
Leadership A team with breadth, depth & energy	A vision that covers both soft and hard factors	Plans that identify: roles, steps, risks, markers and timing
Everyone individuals, roles and groups and their issues		Communications general, two-way, celebrations

These provide a checklist of the topics that will need to be considered both at the start of a change and then throughout the lifecycle and that can be useful at whatever point you start to look at things. These elements need to be clear and any areas of concern within them addressed (or the impact of not doing so worked out). In work situations we have used this sort of checklist as the basis for a meeting of all the involved parties to find out what the situation is and begin to identify what needs to be done and by whom.

Indeed, in more structured organisations these sorts of items form the basis for a risk register where leaders monitor items using a traffic-light system (green – lovely, amber – caution, red – problem). The key, however, is to really probe the topics with questions and get to an accurate understanding of what the situation is under each heading rather than to be able to allocate colours to each heading.

A four-step framework

This framework can provide a guide through the process of change. Effective navigation is important. If strategy is tidy and clean, implementation is definitely dirty and confusing. It is difficult to see where you are and people can quickly get lost (even the leaders).

There are already several different processes and frameworks that can be used to help structure thinking and activity through a change. We have no objection to these and you may find one or another more helpful (Google them if you want to see what they look like). They all provide useful insights that can help leaders think through change. The most prominent are perhaps:

- John Kotter's eight-step process
- Lippitt, Watson and Wesley's seven-stage approach
- Derivations of the Kübler-Ross five-step cycle or Lewin's three-step change
- Prochaska and DiClemente's five-step model (also called the Transtheoretical model)

Our framework is designed as a prompt to think around change in a church situation:

- It is less a top-down approach and more a guide to help think about the timings and categories of action.
- It provides some default steps and strategies that can be discussed and tailored to the particular situation and change.
- It uses an organic metaphor reflecting an essentially human-centred change and highlighting the foundational work needed for effective commitment.

Preparation is something good gardeners seem to understand. It secures the best results. Clearing the weeds, fertilising the ground, choosing seed carefully, timing, planting and watering: these testify to the importance of preparation. This is true with wholehearted change. It takes a lot of preparation and it is essential that the process is, and is seen to be, fair. This helps to maintain unity in Christ, even when there are disagreements. We suggest four steps:

I	Prepare – create the ground ready for change
II	Sow - engage the church
III	Tend - help to realise new outcomes
IV	Harvest - secure the outcomes and benefits

These steps interlock the timings of the external change and the human process of transition in the hearts and minds of people. The first two steps need to be started before the external change. The first needs to be completed before it happens. Beyond this, timing needs to fit with the specifics of the change.

The chart (overleaf) highlights the interlock between change and transition and draws attention to:

- what the leadership team should be focusing on
- how the leaders might go about executing the tasks needed
- potential ideas, and
- one or two watch-outs or things to avoid

It can help to structure actions and provide a checklist that leaders can use to make sure that key elements are not forgotten. It provides some prompts for considering what to do and how to do it.

Good to go?

What do you need to be reasonably confident that you are well organised to lead a change? As a guide, the list would include:

- The goal of the change in terms of a picture or vision of both being and doing that captures the desired destination in a motivational way and highlights what will be different about this future from what the church has at the moment.
- The rationale for doing this, doing it now and doing it this way, with the evidence if needed upon which this is based and the discernment of God's hand in this for the church.
- A clear understanding of how the change will be governed, managed and communicated through its lifecycle.
- The important elements of a plan and, if complex, this should be on paper where it is communicable and provides a checklist.
- This will include the specific goals that sit within the vision and when they are expected to be realised. This needs to be specific enough for people to be clear what needs to be done by when (which is rarely the case with a vision), for people to feel that the tasks to be undertaken are practicable, that the resources and skills needed will be provided and that they will know when these have been realised.
- It will be clear on roles and responsibilities. This will be most realistic and attainable if the planning is done participatively.
- An understanding of whom this will impact in the church and, if appropriate, wider community. What they are likely to feel about this, and how this is to be handled.
- A list of the risks that this involves and how these will be managed.

External change	Before launch	Into and through launch
Transition stage	I	I
Title	Prepare	Sow
'What's' (topics to focus upon)	Build the leadership team Ensure relationships are strong in the church Understand the current reality of the situation Conceive issues, priorities and possibilities Create a readiness for change	Engage the church in the challenges Build readiness for change Test ideas for action and the future Build the vision Create a clear governance model and plan
'How's' (possible actions)	Raise questions and call to prayer Start discussions and reflection Seek ways to test and pilot ideas Formalise the story for a change Define the first steps Define structures & change agents Create a plan Recognise and begin endings to signal moving on	Prayer, debate and purpose – church reflection Explore internal and external community issues (see Appendix) Consider gifts and resources Conceive future (ideas) and challenges Outline steps forward Seize a 'moment of truth' event (as per Chapter 10)
Ideas	Review previous changes – the history Revisit the church 'why?' and build intentionality Explore the cost of inertia and size of prizes Explore 'change readiness'	Consider group by group vs whole church activities Create a church timeline to show continuity and development Facing opposition? – conduct a 'force field' analysis to uncover motives for this across groups Try out elements to build confidence
Watch-outs	Does this have a missional focus? Is the current situation really understood? Don't jump to solutions Beware entrenched groups Are we including all leaders? Remember: conception vs vision	Make sure clear rationale and story Is the process fair? Check soft and hard sides to vision Watch for silent and vocal members Clear next steps?

External change	Underway	Completed
Transition stage	II	II/III
Title	Tend	Harvest
'What's' (topics to focus upon)	Engage all church groups Adapt and revise the vision Communicate creatively and frequently Share the story and progress Celebrate endings and beginnings	Engage all church groups Adapt and revise the vision Share the story and progress Review measures, successes and learnings Look at next steps Transition completion
'How's' (possible actions)	Key events Discussions 1:1, 1:many Open prayer and review Share good news, sad news, stories Mark and celebrate progress Adjust and improve – publicly	Celebrations Discussions 1:1, 1:many Prayer and reviews, measures and reflection Events – review, prayer, learn Revisit vision and think forward
Ideas	Communicate emotions and steps Allocate leaders to prompt for celebration, comms, progress, etc. Use an 'itemised response' (three good things for each one to be improved)	Selective use of stories of personal journeys Use and share reviews of change results Continual update of vision An end-end story Before and after surveys
Watch-outs	Remain engaged with 'opponents' Communication – two-way? frequent? content-rich? Accountability and challenge for outcomes and behaviour Celebrate continuity as well as change	Beware the spring back to past Avoid a winners and losers mentality Watch out for those still struggling Be realistic on progress vs goals (vision is a picture not reality)

With these you are in a good place to embark on change. Indeed, you will have already done so.

Final remarks

In writing this book, we have been conscious of spending time in talking about things that need to be remembered and risks that are being run, and we have provided examples of incidents that can reveal the weaknesses in the way things are handled. This is inevitable in drafting something that aims to help churches to handle change better. But we would be mortified if this reduced the appetite of churches to embrace change.

We believe it is vital that the church follows its missional calling enthusiastically. This will involve change and, we think, more rather than less than we have experienced in the past. The status quo might have been great for the last century, the last decade or even the last year but it is not God's call for now.

With this in mind we offer two final quotes that reflect the importance of seeing what must be done and pressing ahead with it rather than being over-concerned with success or failure:

'Don't aim at success. The more you aim at
it and make it a target, the more you are going to
miss it. For success, like happiness, cannot be
pursued; it must ensue, and it only does as the
unintended side-effect of one's dedication to a
cause greater than oneself or as a by-product of
one's surrender to a person other than oneself."
Victor Frankl, Austrian holocaust survivor

'If you have tried to do something and
failed, you are vastly better off than if you had tried
to do nothing and succeeded.'

Richard M. Stern, novelist

We serve a great God who is calling us to live as his body here on earth and asking us of our best in that mission. We pray that God will bless you as you live out this calling.

The authors

Rod Street

Rod Street coaches individuals and teams through strategic changes. He was previously a partner with PwC where he led the market and customer management practice. He teaches the CPAS Arrow Leadership Programme module on handling change well and works as a CPAS partner. He is married to Carol and they have one son.

His blog site includes further articles and tools and can be found at www.4betterchange.uk.

Rod can be contacted at rodstreet@4betterchange.uk.

Nick Cuthbert

Nick Cuthbert is an author, teacher and evangelist, lay canon and a leader of Lead Academy. He has two children and four grandchildren. He and his wife Lois, are the founding leaders of Riverside Church in Birmingham.

Nick can be contacted at nickc@riverside-church.org.uk

CPAS is an Anglican evangelical mission agency with a vision to develop all kinds of leaders as we enable churches to help every person hear and discover the good news of Jesus Christ.

Our work in this vital area has various different streams to it, from resourcing churches to invest in lay leaders to on-going training for clergy at all stages of their ministry.

Our current areas of ministry include:

Resources for churches

The suite of *Growing Leaders* courses and books help churches make a priority of developing others as leaders, including ready-to-use teaching materials. Courses often run across groups of local churches and participants can include everybody, from long-standing volunteers to those who are identified as having leadership potential.

Other CPAS resources include *Mentoring Matters*, *Growing Through a Vacancy* and more, as well as the Grove Leadership Series of books.

Leadership support

CPAS runs training on key leadership topics, across the UK and Republic of Ireland. We also deliver longer-term initiatives such as the *Arrow Leadership Programme* for leaders aged 25 to 40 who are working in churches or Christian organisations.

Much of CPAS' leadership development work is also delivered in partnership with English dioceses, including year-long leadership programmes, training mentors for clergy and multi-parish benefice learning communities.

Vocations events

CPAS has been running *You and Ministry* weekends for more than 50 years, helping men and women discern whether God is calling them to ordained ministry.

Ventures and Falcon Holidays

Many people take their first steps into leadership on Ventures and Falcon Holidays, led by teams of committed volunteers which welcome more than 4,000 children and young people every year for fun, safe and life-changing holidays across the UK.

Patronage

CPAS is also the largest evangelical patron in the Church of England, with sole or shared responsibility for appointing incumbents to more than 500 benefices nationwide.

To discover more about our work please visit www.cpas.org.uk

Lead Academy uses a distinctive and creative approach to equipping leaders and enabling churches to change in order fulfil their vision.

An 18 month interactive journey using specialized learning communities connects teams of leaders together from similar ministry contexts and the Lead Academy team have now helped a large number of churches of all sizes and denomination to bring about change.

What is involved?

- Two days every six months
- A gathering of 6 - 8 leadership teams joining together
- A mixture of input, team exercises, setting realistic goals for change, fun, interaction and accountability for decisions
- Tackling key issues such as culture change, goal setting, leadership, discipleship and mission
- A controlled but informal environment for teams to benefit from
- Concise but perceptive input from highly regarded leaders around the world

In short, too good to miss!

Who is it for?

Any church that wants to change and move forward towards its God given calling is welcome to apply. Whatever your size or situation we can pair you up with teams similar to your own.

What are church leaders saying who have been through the process?

"For us Lead Academy has proven to be invaluable. Of all the leadership events I have attended this is the one that has given us genuine traction and application back in our church. We have found that Lead Academy has been a real catalyst for bold action and has fired our missional imagination"

"Thanks so much for an absolutely outstanding time at Lead Academy this week. I don't think I've ever been in a setting before where everything we did was so completely focused and relevant for exactly our situation."

"Best of all is the combination of high quality input from the front with ample time with your leadership team to discuss the specific and practical application of that input in your church and parish. Highly recommended."

Find out more and see if there is a community starting soon that you and your team could join?

We would love to help you in any way we can, so do get in touch. For more information visit www.leadacademy.net or contact us at info@leadacademy.net.

Appendix – Landscape of Change

This appendix provides a set of buckets that leaders can use to think through change. It considers all the aspects of the environment, all elements that need to be planned in implementing change, and summary for communicating this. They are summarised in the diagram:

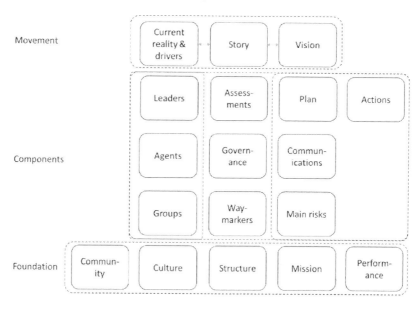

Foundations – why and how to change

The foundations comprise the areas that leaders might look at in order to understand the context for and the priorities for change. The questions to be asked are: What is already there that might shape change? and What might need to change in this area? The answers help explain why change is needed and what shape it might take.

Community

What is the nature of the community that the church serves? What are the needs and opportunities? The unique shape of the local church should reflect and speak into the community that it serves. Changes in the demography, geography, attitudes and activities of the wider community help to set an agenda with which the church needs to align if its ministry is to be relevant.

Culture

What are the values, attitudes and behaviour of the members of the church? Does the church face any of the barriers outlined in Chapter 7? This is a difficult and nebulous area, but it is a significant factor in the health and effective working of a group. Looking at aspects like the warmth of the relationships, the level of commitment to each other, the unity of energy and activity, the presence of cliques or rivalry and the alignment of all aspects of behaviour to God's living are valuable in finding both platforms for change and areas that might be on God's heart for change.

Structure

Are the decision-making structures and forums healthy and effective? Do meeting frequencies, agendas and composition provide effective leadership for the church and any change? Again, are there barriers like those mentioned in Chapter 7? Although the church is a family and can be formal or informal in style, it will still have these structures and they need to be appropriate.

Mission

We have talked about the importance of 'why?' and this bucket is a prompt to check that the pattern of groups, activities, use of money and resources match this why. It is not really about the mission statement. It is an examination of the activity of the church to see how the energy and goals of the church are expressed. Do they match up to what they need to be?

Performance

This is only one of five factors. Nonetheless it is worth including. Sometimes results are a good guide to what is working and what is not, to where there are issues that need to be addressed and to the identifying of root causes that are driving this performance. Performance trends can be the amounts and the composition of money, attendees, members, buildings, staff, etc. What is God blessing? What is not going well?

These five areas provide a broad and outward-facing base for change. It can be helpful not just for leaders but also for the wider church to also have a good appreciation of these.

Sometimes when leaders start to look at these areas they may find that there are already individuals at work changing the situation in one or more of these areas. In a healthy church life this will happen, as people respond to the moving of the Spirit and move things forward without any additional human direction.

Leaders can capitalise on this. Bottom-up initiated change is a powerful force that can help move the community forward quickly if leaders are awake to it.

In one church, the initiative to build the prayer life of the church by using the 24/7 prayer initiative and the creation of a prayer room came entirely bottom-up from someone in the church who became convinced of the importance and opportunity present in getting the church to pray more.

Taking the analysis further might involve engaging in some way with the wider community – civic bodies and community groups, schools, councils, etc. – and talking with these to understand the pressure and issues that they face or see in the area. One of the most powerful and positive tools for change in much consulting work is where the 'voice of the customer' has been allowed to speak into a situation. It often provides a revealing reflection of an organisation and its position in a community that can be difficult to reject and helpful to shape the way forward. Does the community see the church as we would hope they do?

Rick Warren's door-to-door surveying and visiting to shape the ministry of the Sadddleback community reflects a similar philosophy.

Components – what needs organising

The components capture the elements that need to be orchestrated to lead change effectively. On the left of the diagram there are the different groups in church that need to be identified and planned for. At the least, these comprise the following.

Leaders

These are the people who exercise influence within the church, not just people who fill the formal positions of leadership.

Agents

These are individuals who will not just advocate change but will get involved to make things happen and lead the charge on aspects of the change (many may be leaders as well).

Groups

These are the often overlapping clusters of people who together comprise the whole church community (and maybe even some in the wider community, depending on the nature of the change). Thought needs to be given as to how granular a definition of groups (even individuals) is needed and to make sure that a comprehensive list is created.

On the right hand side, there are the most important elements that need to be put in place to enable a change to happen in an ordered fashion. These are key elements that are needed to make change a well-organised process, whether they are done formally or informally.

The plan

This comprises the specific steps that must happen and the sequencing and dependencies that exist between them. This in one sense is a mechanical task that needs to be done. For some changes it will be easy and for others it will be complex. It will help set timelines, responsibilities and resource needs. It is the fundamental of project planning and has some real value even looking at more generalised changes. It will need to include each of the following elements:

Actions

There needs to be clarity over the steps that need to be taken, by whom and by when.

Communications

How will the church be kept up to speed? This needs to address the whole church or community but also should consider the 1:1 or small group discussions that need to take place in order to address the needs of all the important groups within the change.

Main risks and mitigations

What might go wrong with the change and the potential impact? The plan then needs to work out what can be done to mitigate the impact or put in place a failsafe to ensure that the risk is not realised.

The centre column then summarises how the practical and human aspects of the change will be implemented. These will be evident in:

Assessments

These are conducted to decide what needs to be done. These might be church or community surveys, skills audits, research into the demography of the area, or group discussions – essentially anything that is collected to undergird the direction, nature or scope of change.

Governance

A structure that is clear to people. Who is making the decisions, when and how these are going to be made and even the terms of reference. Many controversies occur in church because this is opaque or felt to be illegitimate. People can resist the change or the way that the church is being executed. It is important to minimise unnecessary friction from the latter.

Waymarkers

These mark significant points on the journey through change and show how quickly, successfully and smoothly it is progressing. Ultimately this will also show when the change is deemed to have been completed as well. It can include soft factors (like people feel the service is working well), not just tangible items (like building completed)

Movement – the summary story

The top level of the diagram describes the change: where it is coming from and where it is going to, the rationale, the main factors that are pushing in that direction and the end goal.

These might be summarised in a single document, a 'case for change', that tells the story of what is happening and why. Equally, it might be simply the words that people use to outline the change.

Documents are often produced in larger churches and for building or physical projects but this can also be usefully done for other major changes. It can be a helpful reminder of what is changing and can provoke questions that can help to shape and be built into the change rather than pushed under the surface. Such a summary document can helpfully describe three elements that keep the rationale for changes prominent in the church.

The current reality

How things are at the moment and what are the reasons for the change. Why we need to change this reality.

The vision

Where we are aiming for. How it will be different and better, what the components are and when they are going to be in place.

The story

Joining this all together in a narrative that can be discussed with anyone and can be simply understood and communicated.

Notes

Introduction

1. We recognise that, theologically, being a part of church is not voluntary. However, participation and the nature of it in a local church would seem to us to be self-evidently voluntary for most people, Christians or not.

Chapter 1

1. David R. Brubaker, *Promise and Peril: Understanding and Managing Change and Conflict in Congregations*, Alban Institute, 2009.

Chapter 2

1. See Hebrews 13:8; Malachi 3:6; Job 23:13.
2. See Matthew 18:3; 2 Corinthians 3:18; 2 Peter 3:18; Ephesian 4:15.
3. See Matthew 5:13-16.
4. David Watson, *I Believe in the Church*, Hodder, 1978, p.51.
5. See Acts 7:54 – 8:1.
6. See Acts 5:18.
7. See Acts 6:1-7.
8. See Acts 10:1-23.
9. See Acts 8:26-40.
10. See Acts 16:6-8.
11. See Acts 13:5, 14; 14:1; 16:13; 17:10; 18:7.
12. Alvin Toffler, *Future Shock*, Random House, 1970.
13. Sources for these examples are: *Measuring National Well-being – Households and Families, 2012*, Office for National Statistics, 2012; S. Jivraj, *How has ethnic diversity grown 1991-2001-2011?*, University of Manchester, 2012; 'British Social Attitudes 30', NatCen, 2013; www.statistics.gov.uk; data.gov.uk, 'Social Trends';

'The Communications Market 2014', Ofcom; Richard Wilkinson and Kate Pickett, *The Spirit Level*, Penguin, 2010.

Chapter 3

1. See 1 Corinthians 1:10-17; 3:1-22; Philippians 4:2-3; Romans 14:1-12.
2. See Romans 14:1-12; Ephesians 5:21; Galatians 2:1-14.
3. *Global CEO Appointments*, High Pay Centre, 2012.
4. J. P. Meyer and L. Herscovitch, 'Commitment in the Workplace', *Human Resource Management Review*, 11(3), 2001.
5. See 2 Samuel 24:24.
6. Gallup, *State of the Global Workplace*, 2013.

Chapter 4

1. Kurt Lewin, 'Frontiers in Group Dynamics: Concept, Method and Reality in Social Science; Social Equilibria and Social Change', *Human Relations*, June 1947.
2. William Bridges, *Transitions: Making Sense of Life's Changes*, Da Capo Press, 2004.
3. Mary Schmich, 'Advice, like youth, probably just wasted on the young', *Chicago Tribune*, 1 June 1997.

Chapter 5

1. See 1 Corinthians 12:12-31.
2. Chris Argyris and Donald A. Schön, *Theory in Practice: Increasing Professional Effectiveness*, Jossey-Bass, 1974; or for a more accessible explanation see http://www.slideshare.net/mrnelson/chris-argyris-4903367 or http://www.slideshare.net/fib74/double-loop-reasoning
3. Ronald A. Heifetz, *Leadership without Easy Answers*, Harvard University Press, 1994.
4. See Ephesians 4:1-16 and the picture of unity provided here.
5. See John 21:15-25.

6. William Oncken, *Managing Management Time: Who's Got the Monkey?*, Prentice Hall, 1985.

7. For example, see John 8:1-11; Luke 18:18-30; John 21:15-25.

8. See Jesus on judging (Luke 6:37-42), his response to the criticism of accepting his feet being anointed (Luke 7:36-50), his challenge to the Sadducees (Matthew 22:23-33), his story of the good Samaritan in response to a question on the law (Luke 10:25-37) or his challenge to the lawyers about healing on the Sabbath (Luke 14:1-6). He acted without fear and with directness, humour, challenge and stories that show how confident he was in himself and clear about what he thought.

9. David R. Brubaker, *Promise and Peril: Understanding and Managing Change and Conflict in Congregations*, Alban Institute, 2009.

10. For instance, John P. Kotter, *Leading Change*, Harvard Business Review Press, 1996; John P. Kotter and Dan S. Cohen, *Heart of Change: Real-Life Stories of How People Change Their Organizations*, Harvard Business Review Press, 2012.

11. Emmy E. Werner and Ruth S. Smith. *Overcoming the Odds: High Risk Children from Birth to Adulthood*, Cornell University Press, 1992, p.192.

12. The burning platform analogy developed from the frightening experience of the Piper Alpha disaster in the North Sea in July 1988 when a fireball engulfed the oil rig, killing 167 men. The only survivors were those who ignored one of the cardinal rules of survival at sea – by jumping into the water.

Chapter 6

1. Simon Sinek, *Start With Why: How Great Leaders Inspire Everyone to Take Action*, Penguin, 2011.

2. Michael Fullan, *Leading in a Culture of Change*, Jossey-Bass, 2001.

3. See Psalm 127:1.

4. See Matthew 28:19.

5. Diana Butler Bass, *The Practicing Congregation: Imagining a New Old Church*, Alban Institute, 2004.

Chapter 7

1. R. Paul Stevens and Phil Collins, *The Equipping Pastor: A Systems Approach to Congregational Leadership*, Alban Institute, 1993, p.37.
2. See 1 Corinthians 3:6; 2 Corinthians 9:10; Philippians 1:6.
3. Charles Handy, *The Empty Raincoat: Making Sense of the Future*, Random House, 1993.
4. Robin Dunbar, see http://en.wikipedia.org/wiki/Dunbars_number
5. *From Anecdote to Evidence: Findings from the Church Growth Research Programme 2011-2013*, www.churchgrowthresearch.org.uk
6. Rt Revd James Newcome, Bishop of Carlisle at a multi-benefice training day in 2013.
7. http://insidenorthpoint.org/practically-speaking/
8. See Acts 1:23-26; 9:15-19.
9. See Acts 6:1-7.
10. See Acts 15:12-29.
11. See Acts 17:16-23.

Chapter 8

1. There are many examples of teamwork: even Moses took the advice from Jethro (Exodus 18:24-26); Jesus selected the disciples to work alongside him (Mark 3:13-14); Paul operated in teams at Antioch (Acts 13:1), with Barnabas (Acts 11:26). The early church worked in this way, from the apostles' behaviour to the selection of the seven (Acts 6:1-7) and the repeated mention of elders in the church (Acts 11:30; 14:23; 15:22; 20:17).
2. The Arrow research is based on a pre-module questionnaire that yielded 139 concerns from over 80 leaders between 2009 and 2013.

4. David R. Brubaker, *Promise and Peril: Understanding and Managing Change and Conflict in Congregations*, Alban Institute, 2009.
5. James M. Kouzes and Barry Z. Posner, *The Leadership Challenge*, Jossey-Bass, 1987.
6. John J. Gabarro, *The Dynamics of Taking Charge*, Harvard Business School Press, 1987.
7. See Matthew 20:20-28; Mark 10:35-45.
8. See John 8:1-11; Luke 18:18-25.
9. See Acts 5:1-11.
10.   http://en.wikipedia.org/wiki/Greshams_law
11. Jim Herrington, Mike Bonem, James H. Furr, *Leading Congregational Change*, Jossey-Bass, 2000.

Chapter 9

1. Dorothy L. Sayers, *Mind of the Maker*, Methuen, 1941.
2. Les Robinson, www.enablingchange.co.au
3. Howard Gardner, *Changing Minds: The Art and Science of Changing Our Own and Other People's Minds*, Harvard Business School Press, 2004.
4. John J. Gabarro, *The Dynamics of Taking Charge*, Harvard Business School Press, 1987.

Chapter 10

1. Barry Oshry, *Seeing Systems: Unlocking the Mysteries of Organizational Life*, Berrett-Koehler, 2007.
2. Malcolm Gladwell, *The Tipping Point: How Little Things Can Make a Big Difference*, Abacus, 2002, p.56ff.

Chapter 11

1. James Brian Quinn, *Strategies for Change: Logical Incrementalism*, Irwin, 1980.
2. See John 17:20-23.

3. See 1 Corinthians 12:12-31.

4. See Ephesians 4:2-6.

5. Daryl R. Conner, *Managing at the Speed of Change: How Resilient Managers Succeed and Prosper Where Others Fail*, John Wiley & Sons, 1997.

Chapter 12

1. John P. Kotter and Dan S. Cohen, *Heart of Change: Real-Life Stories of How People Change Their Organizations*, Harvard Business Review Press, 2012, p.ix.

2. This refers to Edward de Bono's six thinking hats (see http://en.wikipedia.org/wiki/Six_Thinking_Hats), where the black hat asks the wearer to identify reasons to be cautious and conservative.

Chapter 13

1. See for instance http://www.ssireview.org/blog/entry/fail_faster_succeed_sooner /

2. (IBM IBV global survey of 1500 practitioners, 2008): The most significant challenges were changing mind-sets and attitudes 58%, culture 49%, underestimated complexity 35%, resource shortages 33%, lack of senior management commitment 32%. (Economist Intelligence Unit (EIU), 600 executive interviews, 2008): Core issues are winning hearts and minds, generating buy-in and cultural challenges, i.e. handling the people issues. Here the problem identified around change is the failure to address the risks it brings to people. (EIU survey of 300 executives and middle management executives, 2010): The biggest causes of failure were 36-28% poor planning, 17-25% lack of senior management commitment, 14-16% poor communications, and 15-10% employee resistance. The percentage spreads reflect senior vs middle views, which is interesting in itself.

Chapter 14

1. Jean Paul Lederach, *Reconcile: Conflict Transformation for Ordinary Christians*, Herald Press, 2014, p.61ff.
2. See, for instance, Acts 6:1-2; 11:2-3; 15:36-41; 1 Corinthians 1:10-7; Philippians 4:2-3.
3. See James 2:1-7 for fairness or Matthew 18:1-14 for treatment of the weaker party.
4. David R. Brubaker, *Promise and Peril: Understanding and Managing Change and Conflict in Congregations*, Alban Institute, 2009, p.110.
5. John P. Kotter and Leonard A. Schlesinger, 'Choosing Strategies for Change', *Harvard Business Review*, 1979.

Chapter 15

1. D. Buchanan, Louise Fitzgerald, D. Ketley, R. Gollop, J. L. Jones, S. S. Lamont, A. Neath and E. Whitby, 'Not going back, a review of the literature on sustaining organizational change', *International Journal of Management Reviews*, 2005, 7(3).

Chapter 16

1. www.strategyand.pwc.com
2. Edgar H. Schein, *Organizational Culture and Leadership*, Jossey-Bass, 1992. See also, Edgar H. Schein, 'Organizational Culture', Sloan School of Management, MIT Working Papers, 1988, link http://hdl.handle.net/1721.1/2224
3. http://www.forbes.com/sites/alastairdryburgh/2014/10/28/memo-to-the-ceo-stop-talking-about-culture/
4. http://www.ceoinstitute.com/resources/ceos-desk/blog-article/creating-culture-change/
5. Frances Hesselbein, 'The Key to Cultural Transformation', *Leader to Leader*, Spring 1999; http://blogs.hbr.org/2013/12/theres-no-such-thing-as-a-culture-turnaround/;

http://developingchurches.ning.com/profiles/blogs/odbulletin-1-2014-where-is-od-going

Chapter 17

1. Jim Collins, *Good to Great*, Random House, 2001, Chapter 4.

For Further Reading

The following books and articles are highlighted for those who might wish to read more deeply into different aspects mentioned in the book. This is not designed as a comprehensive list on the topics but, rather, sources that we would suggest might be good starting points to dig deeper.

The human process of transition

Bridges, W., *Transitions: Making Sense of Life's Changes*, Da Capo Press, 2004.

Bridges, W., *Managing Transitions: Making the Most of Change*, Nicholas Brealey, 1991.

Gardner, H., *Changing Minds: The Art and Science of Changing Our Own and Other People's Minds*, Harvard Business School Press, 2004.

Johnson, S., *Who Moved My Cheese?*, Random House, 1999.

Oshry, B., *Seeing Systems: Unlocking the Mysteries of Organizational Life*, Berrett-Koehler, 1995.

Personal skills

Coutu, D., 'How Resilience Works', *Harvard Business Review*, May 2002.

Covey, S., *The 7 Habits of Highly Effective People*, Simon & Schuster, 1989.

Friedman, E. H., *Generation to Generation: Family Process in Church and Synagogue*, Guildford Press, 1985.

Friedman, E. H., *A Failure of Nerve*, Seabury Books, 2007.

Kline, N., *Time to Think*, Ward Lock, 1999.

MacDonald, G., *A Resilient Life*, Thomas Nelson, 2004.

Patterson, K., Grenny, J., McMillan, R. and Switzler, A., *Crucial Conversations, Tools for Talking when Stakes are High*, McGraw-Hill, 2012.

Quinn, R. E., *Deep Change: Discovering the Leader Within*, Jossey-Bass, 1996.

Seligman, M., 'Building Resilience', *Harvard Business Review*, April 2011.

Stone, D., Patton, B. and Heen, S., *Difficult Conversations*, Penguin, 1999.

The change process

Essawi, M. and Tilchin, O., 'Adaptive Collaboration Model for Organizational Change', *American Journal of Industrial and Business Management*, 2012, 2, pp.145-152.

Fritz, R., *The Path of Least Resistance*, Butterworth-Heinemann, 1984.

Fritz, R., *Creating*, Butterworth-Heinemann, 1991.

Kotter, J. P. and Cohen, D. S., *The Heart of Change*, Harvard Business School Press, 2002.

Kotter, J. P., *Leading Change*, Harvard Business School Press, 1996.

Newton, R., *Managing Change Step by Step*, Prentice Hall, 2007.

Leadership in change

Fullan, M., *Leading in a Culture of Change*, Jossey-Bass, 2007.

Gabarro, J. J., *The Dynamics of Taking Charge*, Harvard Business School Press, 1987.

Kotter, J. P., *The Leadership Factor*, Free Press, 1988.

Kotter, J. P., 'Managing Yourself: How to save good ideas', *Harvard Business Review*, October 2010.

Kouzes, J. and Posner, B., *The Leadership Challenge*, Jossey-Bass, 1995.

Kouzes, J. and Posner, B., *Christian Reflections on the Leadership Challenge*, Jossey-Bass, 2006.

Quigley, J. V., *Vision: How Leaders Develop it, Sustain It, & Share It*, McGraw-Hill, 1993.

Smith, D. M., *Divide or Conquer: How Great Teams turn Conflict into Strength*, Portfolio, 2008.

Culture

Katzenbach, J., Steffen, I. and Kronley, C., 'Cultural Change That Sticks', *Harvard Business Review*, July/August 2012.

Schein, E. H., *Organizational Culture and Leadership*, Jossey-Bass, 1985.

Systems thinking

Handy, C., *The Empty Raincoat: Making Sense of the Future*, Random House, 1993.

Senge, P. M., *The Fifth Discipline*, Random House, 1990.

Conflict

Christensen, C., Marx, M. and Stevenson, H., 'The Tools of Cooperation and Change', *Harvard Business Review*, 2006.

Kotter, J. P. and Schlesinger, L. A., 'Choosing Strategies for Change', Harvard Business Review, 2008.

Lederach, J. P., *Reconcile: Conflict Transformation for Ordinary Christians*, Herald Press, 2014.

The church and change

Brubaker, D. R., *Promise and Peril: Understanding and Managing Change and Conflict in Congregations*, The Alban Institute, 2009.

Coutts, P., *Choosing Change: How to Motivate Churches to Face the Future*, Rowman & Littlefield, 2013.

Elford, K., *Creating the Future of the Church: A Practical Guide to Addressing Whole-System Change*, SPCK, 2013.

Herrington, J., Bonem, M. and Furr, J. II., *Leading Congregational Change*, Jossey-Bass, 2000.

Stevens, R. P. and Collins, P., *The Equipping Pastor*, The Alban Institute, 1993.

Warren, R., *The Purpose Driven Church: Growth Without Compromising Your Message & Mission*, Zondervan, 1995.

Watson, D., *I Believe in the Church*, Hodder & Stoughton, 1982.

Woods, C. J., *Congregational Megatrends*, The Alban Institute, 1996.